India: The Wrong Transition

India: The Wrong Transition

Anand K Sahay

AAKAR

India: The Wrong Transition
Anand K Sahay

First Published 2019

ISBN 978-93-5002-614-4

•

Published by
AAKAR BOOKS
28 E Pocket IV, Mayur Vihar Phase I
Delhi 110 091 India
aakarbooks@gmail.com

Laser Typeset at
Arpit Printographers, Delhi

Printed at
Sapra Brothers, Noida

for my daughter Mimansa–*artist and sea diver–*
whose world is a great expanse

Contents

KASHMIR

Preface

This is a collection of my articles written on a steady basis over the past five years. These writings are mostly about the ways of Prime Minister Narendra Modi's government (2014-19), RSS-BJP's ideological underpinnings which shaped the government's actions, and the response these elicited within the political system. 'Far & Near', my monthly column in Asian Age and the Deccan Chronicle, forms the backbone of the book, but many articles are from elsewhere.

I have tried to write with a sense of freedom, but this has not always been feasible, given the temper of the times. Nevertheless, the media platforms that gave me the hospitality of their columns were good enough to offer leeway. For this I express my gratitude.

The names of all the publications where these articles first appeared are duly acknowledged. I wrote to each, outlining my purpose to gather my writings in a collection. None expressed any reservation.

I believe these writings constitute a unity, and offer a glimpse into the contemporary history of India as they attempt to explain the times we have lived through- to fellow Indians and to external observers.

The book has three sections—on the general political situation in the country, on Kashmir, and on India's relations with neighbours and the rest of the world. It wasn't planned this way. I just wrote on issues of interest to me as they arose, and found they quite neatly fitted into three boxes. I have subjected some of the published articles to very light language editing.

I wish to record here my appreciation of Gulzar Ahmad Bhat, a young friend from Kashmir who is a fine journalist and research scholar. His help in locating many of the articles from the Internet was inestimable. This project would have been stymied but for his timely rescue act.

Journalism is a solo effort and a collaborative effort at the same time. New Delhi has many journalists of substance. These have been difficult times for them to do their work in relative freedom, and yet there can be no restraint imposed on pre-publication informal exchanges of ideas, information, and interpretations between practitioners of this trade, which is a deadly serious calling as it involves crossing swords with those in authority and accepting the attendant risks. My heartfelt thanks to journalist friends from whom I have picked up information, rumour, gossip or conflicting interpretation as a stepping stone to shaping my own perspective.

29 March, 2019 **Anand K Sahay**
New Delhi

Introduction

In the past five years, since the advent of Prime Minister Narendra Modi on the scene, India finds itself in the throes of messy developments* and institutional subversion.

The RSS-BJP may hope these add up to a transition that can be taken forward to transform India into the land of their dreams. Outside this group inclined to pray for the success of *Hindutva*, or political Hinduism, the work toward such a transition is unlikely to send hopes soaring. This suggests that many social and political battles "for the soul of India" lie ahead, no matter who forms the next government in India.

For votaries of the special genus called *Hindu Rashtra*, or a Hindu-supremacist re-ordering of India that can only be brought about through a denigration of the core values of India's present Constitution, relative success in the near-term of the experiment begun under Modi depends crucially on the BJP returning to power after May 23—when the poll result for parliament is due—with a majority of its own, as in 2014.

Should this fail to materialise, the sustained work done for the *Hindutva* cause under the leadership of the current prime minister is at risk of dissipating, though ideological battles will not cease.

A BJP-led coalition government, but one in which the present ruling party no longer independently commands a majority in the directly elected lower chamber, is unlikely to be able to continue with the present agenda of the RSS-BJP, which the Modi regime assiduously attempted to give effect to within the constraints it faced. At least, it is not likely to be able to do so at the same pace as the Modi government.

The past five years have been very special for the politico-religious far right in India associated with the country's religious majority. This element has gained the opportunity to build a scaffolding on which to fabricate an edifice of a certain type. Such a prospect had not been yielded when the late Atal Behari Vajpayee, the first prime minister from the RSS-BJP fold, came to office in the late 1990s.

The demolition of a medieval mosque in Ayodhya in 1992 under the aegis of the RSS, the fount of *Hindu Rashtra* inspiration which has spawned dozens of ideologically spirited outfits that do not balk at violence, and the simultaneous movement to build a Ram temple where the mosque had stood, had helped turn the BJP into a mass party. For the first time this Rightist force was able to extend its reach into northern India's hinterland and could, on the basis of provocative pseudo-religious slogans, successfully tap into the votes of non-privileged Hindu caste groups—the OBCs (intermediate caste groups categorised as such on the basis of educational and social backwardness), and the dalit (the former untouchables of Hindu society) sections.

This was great going for a party that was grounded in upper-caste, Hindu elite, histories and traditions which it sought to present as India's national values that were at the core of Indian culture. But the tendency had not been forceful enough to give the BJP of those years a parliamentary majority of its own.

Prime Minister Vajpayee was hemmed in by coalition partners who were of the "secular" persuasion—they didn't share RSS-BJP's *Hindutva* thinking and its goal of *Hindu Rashtra* but had opportunistically chosen to be part of government so as not to miss out on the loaves and fishes of office.

Modi, in contrast, coming ten years after the Vajpayee government was defeated in the national election of 2004, has faced no such constraints. This is on account of his sweeping Lok Sabha strength, although from time to time his government did confront difficulties and could not effect massive change by amending the Constitution as it did not have a majority in the Rajya Sabha, the Upper House of parliament.

In the Modi period, the RSS-BJP were helped by a key factor. Their main ideological and political rival on the national stage, the Congress party, which has been in office for about three fourths of the time since independence from British rule in 1947, and was largely instrumental in creating the template of post-colonial India, had an insignificant presence in the Lok Sabha.

It had fared poorly in the parliamentary poll of 2014, although in the preceding ten years the two governments it led gave strong economic growth on a decadal average basis, lifted more people out of poverty than any other government in a comparable time frame, passed important legislation in the field of citizens' right to information, and created what is arguably the world's largest guaranteed rural employment scheme for the poorest sections.

But the Congress party's leadership appeared watery and uncharismatic. Its organisation had weakened visibly. These had caused its influence in the public sphere to erode over time. Also, for many- though this factor should not be over-stated in India's context- the Congress had come to be associated with dynasts.

This was seen to be at odds with what is sometimes called "aspirational India", the young segment of the population which has existential reasons to hope and lays greater stress on presumed merit than on any other principle to advance societal and national goals and—importantly—is thought to be impatient with any mention of "socialism", even of the "democratic" variety, which the Congress, going back to the Nehru years, delineated.

What's more, while Congress' credo—which emphasised pluralism, personal liberties, democracy, a programmatic inclination to raise the lives of the needy through state intervention and balanced regional development, and placed a premium on autonomy of action in the world arena-remained more or less intact, in practice more was expected of the "the party of freedom" to stand up for its core beliefs.

In 2014, the very idea of the Congress— and the "idea of India" that it espoused and which is enshrined in our Constitution—proved no match for a rampaging RSS-BJP under the command of Modi.

In his election campaign for the Lok Sabha five years ago, the man who would be prime minister formally proclaimed a broad-spectrum persona to attract all, harnessed the energy of the unsuspecting youth by promising jobs and a bright future (the *achche din* slogan), dog-whistled his way into the hearts of the communal-minded Hindu who finds merit in the idea of disadvantaging the religious minorities, comprehensively won over the Hindu traditionalist, and also paved a path to reach the votaries of the market-alone principle by promising "maximum governance, minimum government".

Modi also projected for himself a larger-than-life figure-that of a true "great leader" in whose hands the country would be safe, a man of the masses who had risen to the top through hard work and was a "nationalist" to the core. By this, of course, he meant a "Hindu nationalist", his description of himself in a Reuters interview in the run-up to the 2014 election which earned him plaudits from his expanding constituency. This set up a contrast with "Indian nationalist". India was evidently changing.

Many loved the "New India"—Modi's coinage—that was unfolding under the 'great leader', but serious fears too came to be expressed. The principal characteristic of the governing dispensation turned out to be too much talk, too little action, and considerable action with negative consequences for society.

The poor got little out of it, the owning classes didn't feel they were supported, the unemployed youth were adrift, the farmers seemed to lose hope, and there was violence against Muslims and Christians (mainly the former), against the dalit community, against journalists and intellectuals if they didn't fall in line, and against the very idea of dissent. Alongside, hocus-pocus from Hindu mythology—peddled as the acme of scientific glory in Hindu India—was passionately projected. This has led Hyderabad-based social scientist Kancha Ilaiah to suggest that the Modi government has promoted "primitivism".

And yet—such was the scale of the support from a craven media, especially television—Modi, in opinion polls that are routinely published on God knows what basis, remains India's most trusted leader, the safest pair of hands in the country to take us to "glory", to take us to the point where India will be acclaimed as *vishwa guru* or teacher to the world—which is actually a demand put forth by the current RSS chief, Mohan Bhagwat.

So disappointing have been the results of government policy in the past five years, the famous journalist-author Arun Shourie, who once edited one of India's finest newspapers and was afterward a minister in the Vajpayee cabinet, asked with acuity, "There is a lot of sizzle, but where's the steak?"

To overcome such criticism, the regime has taken self-serving propaganda to absurd limits, and amusingly its all-round failures have been laid at the door of its opponents (voted out five years earlier), thanks to the media flagrantly acting at the regime's behest.

Why did mainstream media in India- honourable exceptions apart—abandon the practice of journalism in the Modi raj can be the subject of fruitful scholarly research, but what one hears in journalist circles is mortifying. A sting operation last year showed that the *crème de la crème* of Indian journalism were only too willing, for a suitable price, to let poisonous *Hindutva* propaganda prevail in their news columns.

The penetration of social media and television has increased in India by leaps and bounds in recent years. Social media has been used to spread hate and intolerance against whole communities, and against critics, through what appears to be a carefully orchestrated programme of action that involves thousands of foot soldiers. And, mainstream media has succumbed, by and large. Together social media and conventional media have worked to magnify the government's and the RSS-BJP's message, and lampooned their opponents.

If the media had stuck to its job, the Modi government is likely to have been running for cover. It is, in fact, plausible to argue that while the Modi government is no doubt a creature of RSS ideology and organisation, it may have found it difficult to establish itself if it weren't for the fawning media, which was responsible for the building of the Modi persona.

In the absence of institutional restraint, and of independent journalism, which is not afraid to excavate the wrong-doings of the rulers and expose the mechanism through which their dark deeds are performed, democracy in India can today be said to be on the brink of a precipice. It has never been laid so low before, though there have been bad times for democracy in the past and unedifying policy failures.

The Modi government has been unlike any other government India has known. Its actions show that it has been ideology-driven in the extreme, and has limited inclination for the material development of society—which is serious, dogged, time-consuming, business. Its aim appears to be no less than the transformation of both state and society in India along prescriptive religious lines through the misuse of state power.

This has been sought to be done not only through governmental effort and public funds, but also the odious organised actions of a cadre of tens of thousands of persons outside of government—akin to a paramilitary force in civvies-who resort to physical violence and threats, the dissemination of fake news to achieve narrow political and ideological ends, and intense activity on social media to vilify, abuse and threaten opponents, all the while uttering traditional Hindu pieties.

This is their path to force their imagined Hindu way of life upon the country, with "force" being the operative word. The great, all-knowing, leader, who sits at the top of the pyramid, guides and inspires the 'virtuous'. But he gives no succour to the poor; his solace is reserved for plutocrats. To cement his place, he must purvey false narratives of nationalism and resort to militaristic rhetoric.

The pages that follow are a compilation of opinion articles by the present writer published in newspapers and on current affairs portals, and are a chronicle of our times. They constitute a sustained journalistic scrutiny of Modi raj. They offer an interpretation of events as these unfolded, and a critique of some terrible things to which we have been witness in this country, above all the vanity and the vainglorious ways of those who rode a public mandate to give us democratic governance but wilfully served other-disturbing- agendas.

---

* For a recent clear-eyed view of Hindu communalism, see Amrita Basu, *Violent Conjunctures in Democratic India*, Cambridge University Press, first published 2015, South Asia edition 2016.

'SECOND REPUBLIC' & OTHER STORIES

In 2019, BJP Goes Back to Its Old RSS Roots

There is an unmistakable contrast between the atmosphere generated by the BJP-RSS in the Lok Sabha election five years ago, spearheaded by a man who would soon be Prime Minister, and the poll campaign of the ruling dispensation for the Parliament election which is less than a month away.

When he was BJP's candidate for the top job, Modi emphasised development, promised to create two crore jobs a year, root out corruption and black money, and create an atmosphere of equal opportunity for all to succeed in life through the mantra of *sabka saath, sabka vikas*.

On this basis, the connect with the voter was instant, and paid rich electoral dividend, for the first time catapulting the BJP to a position where it could have a parliamentary majority of its own, although NDA allies were included in the governing architecture.

The future PM appeared to consciously obscure from view the majoritarian outlook for which the RSS and its kindred outfits—the BJP included—are generally known.

Although Modi had been a full-time volunteer of the RSS—a *pracharak*—before he became Chief Minister of Gujarat, he was all too aware that if he had to achieve his goal of heading the government at the Centre he had to pitch his appeal to the whole country, not to a particular section.

Thus were mobilised farmers, workers, the middle classes in their broadest definition, and businesses, besides all caste and religion groups, and the youth everywhere. With the help of a fawning media, the sense was created that freedom from constraints was round the corner. The BJP's stunning win that followed whipped other parties, especially the Congress.

Contentious issues like the Ram temple at Ayodhya, scrapping of Article 370 of the Constitution which links Kashmir to India under the Instrument of Accession signed in 1947, and RSS' jingoistic nationalism (*Hindutva*) were kept away from view.

So successful was the technique that it resulted in a Modi wave which swept everything before it, and the vote for the BJP was densely packed. While the party won only about 31 per cent of the votes nationally, voting in its favour was a lot more concentrated in north India, besides Gujarat and Maharashtra, than the national data might suggest. In these places, the saffron share of the votes polled rose for the first time in history above even 40 per cent.

In 2019, however, the BJP appears to be returning to its roots, switching tactics completely. In focus for it now are the middle classes including the small urban trader, and the upper caste of Hindu society, not the broad spectrum of all Indians, like in 2014. These particular sections have been the RSS-BJP's traditional catchment area, the segment on which it used to bank before it became a mass party in 1992.

The new emphasis on RSS-BJP's old configuration may be seen in the government's move to extend the benefit of reservations in government employment and college admissions at public institutions to the "general" category, and surprisingly embraced even those who paid income tax.

This of course made a mockery of the idea of affirmative action, which had been conceived as a measure of social justice to help historically deprived sections of society who were handicapped on account of societal discrimination- namely the SCs, STs and the OBCs. Evidently, wooing voters took precedence over principle.

Besides playing the reservation card for the upper caste, the government raised the floor for paying income tax nearly three times—to people whose monthly earnings were around Rs. 60,000 per month, a category which, in the Indian context, counts as well-to-do. In India, governments have tried hard to bring more and more people into the tax net, but this was a step in the opposite direction.

Bending over backwards to please the middle classes and the upper caste became necessary because the poorer strata—the SC, ST and the OBCs, who were recent converts to the BJP's cause—had begun to chafe at the bit. The five years of the present dispensation have impacted the poorest sections of India the hardest.

These were not traditional BJP voters, but the party was able to make inroads into this group through communal mobilisation with its successful campaign to demolish Ayodhya's Babri mosque in 1992. A consolidation of this gain on an unprecedented scale was achieved with the seeming broad-church approach of Modi in 2014. It is this architecture that has now come under inordinate pressure, especially among the younger people—both urban and rural.

The component of BJP's support base enticed in more recent times has felt disregarded on account of adverse policy in the past five years. Unemployment has raged in the country with the present situation being the worst in 45 years, and farmers' woes have worsened, the glitzy propaganda notwithstanding. Things have got to such a point that the government finds it expedient not to publish crucial labour bureau data and data in other key economic fields, raising doubts for the first time in India's history about the integrity of official statistics. The acting chairman of the National Statistical Commission has resigned.

With the poorer sections feeling let down, it became a matter of practical necessity for the government party to return the focus to the middle classes and the upper caste, a section likely to be more sympathetic. In a sense, from having lately become a multi-class and multi-caste party, a bit like the Congress, the BJP has been forced to resile and return to its uni-class past. Structurally, this renders it more vulnerable than at any time in the past two decades.

In order not to be overwhelmed by the situation, the saffron party is trying to place its bets on two unknowns. The first is the orator-doer persona of the Prime Minister, though this wasn't of much avail when the BJP lost the Assembly election in three Hindi-belt states, considered its forte, late last year.

The second is the venting of strident nationalism after Balakot in order to appear attractive once again to the relatively poorer sections, who have otherwise got little from the system. BJP's opponents would, in fact, hope that the saffron party will persists with ultra-nationalism and pseudo-patriotism while they themselves get to highlight questions of daily life of the poor.

The governing party would no doubt hope that it can come good in the Lok Sabha election in spite of its present beleaguered status if, in multi-cornered contests, its opponents cut one another down and do not threaten it in unison. In that event, it will need to ensure that it does not bleed upper caste-middle class votes, the sections it is critically relying on in northern India, its corps headquarters.

Asian Age & Deccan Chronicle, 19 March, 2019

Balakot and After, or How to Build a Strategic Doctrine for Political Gain

Oh, What a Lovely War!

The landmark 1969 musical, director Richard Attenborough's debut film—a satire on the First World War, and on war and war-mongering— has even the Dalai Lama blessing the military effort in the early part of the epic comedy, so pious seems the project, so plainly just.

In India, the storyline has not been dissimilar. The messianic effort by the ruling establishment that has gone into underlining the justness of the cause and the absolute necessity of the Balakot airstrikes—in weeks before a national election—has had many mesmerised.

The effect can be felt even a fortnight after the event, although it is unclear if the spell will last until polling day. The prime minister is sitting pretty, very pleased with his war-like manoeuvres which may fetch him extra votes. This could make up for anticipated vote-loss on account of shoddy governance and lofty disregard of the interests of the poorer sections—a wide swathe on the demographic map.

Ironically, Pakistan's prime minister is sitting pretty too, savouring the adulation of the faithful. It appears that everyone is pleased with Pulwama and its after-effect. Balakot has turned out not to be a zero-sum game in which only one of two sides gains.

Indeed, Balakot was India's crescendo moment with our Mirage 2000s crossing the line and raining down smart explosives (whose results in human casualties, if any, are unknown).

Pakistan's high-point was not long in coming as its F-16s returned the compliment mid-morning a day later by violating our airspace in broad daylight—the Indian Air Force jets had spooked the Pakistanis when it was pitch dark—and discharging ordnance in the open grounds of a military compound near the border, just to make their point.

We said we hit a terrorist training camp of the Jaish-e-Mohammed, and it was not our intention to attack the Pakistani military. But the Pakistanis were having none of this. In their reply, they hit our military. More than tit for tat accomplished.

One fighter plane lost on each side, but that's small beer. For Pakistan a pilot lost, for India a pilot captured and swiftly returned in a grand "gesture of peace".

Narendra Modi had his "revenge" for Pulwama (although he was shooting a film in Corbett National Park when the CRPF jawans fell in southern Kashmir and reportedly didn't stop filming). Just weeks before the Lok Sabha election, this was really all he was after.

Less than a fortnight later, he would tell an Ahmedabad election rally in his native Gujarat that it is "in my nature to settle scores, and to chase and beat you up inside your own home". In this vulgarity of prime ministerial expression, there was verbal chest-thumping and self-valorisation. In the theatrics of that moment, the Indian Air Force had not even an incidental role to play.

Imran Khan, on the other hand, is also brimming with satisfaction, with the British press praising his statesmanlike action in returning a prisoner of war without any fuss so as not to escalate hostilities, and one of his ministers declaring that his leader deserved the Nobel prize for peace for showing forbearance in a moment of military tumult (between nuclear-armed neighbours with a long history of fighting).

The score pretty much even on both sides, the high commissioners of India and Pakistan have returned to their posts after having earlier left for home "for consultations". New Delhi is now even said to be giving thought to receiving a Pakistani delegation to work out details for the construction of a corridor through Pakistani territory so that Indian pilgrims may visit the Kartarpur Saheb gurudwara, one of the holiest Sikh shrines very close to the border. Just as well, of course. Better jaw-jaw, than war-war.

We limped back to the India-Pakistan normal in three days flat. So, what's changed? What has been gained, other than election propaganda mileage for Modi? Observers are rightly confused.

But not our all-knowing 'strategic community', the gaggle of retired foreign service bureaucrats and military officials with ageing moustaches, who breathe fire and brimstone when it comes to Pakistan, hector other neighbours but advise caution in dealing with China, and recommend straightforward obsequiousness in interacting with the United States—exactly the sort of counsel Modi values.

These experts tell us that in bombing Balakot, we have drawn a new red line, that a new strategic doctrine has been revealed, that a no-nonsense posture has now been adumbrated in relation to Pakistan. Which is what exactly? That each time a terrorist incident of some magnitude occurs in Kashmir or elsewhere, our fighter-jets will be taxiing for takeoff to hit targets inside Pakistan?

Given the record since 2015, that means about twice a year on average, in some years may be three times. The way the Pakistani F-16s tore into our airspace just the day after Balakot (luckily there were no casualties on the ground to complicate the strategic picture), skirmishes possibly leading to a full-scale military conflagration may be on the cards about three times a year.

How is that for a strategic doctrine for nuclear-armed neighbours in the shadow of India's "no first-use" nuclear doctrine meant to underline our peaceable temperament before a world audience of doubting Toms?

Another thought for our less-than-reticent strategic experts who flaunt their wares before breathless television anchors: how might an unconstrained Pakistan have reacted to an uninvited Indian incursion into its airspace if the Americans had not been negotiating with Islamabad to assist with the Taliban talks prior to a probable US withdrawal from Afghanistan?

Modi has proved a red-hot, election-time, hyper-nationalist. We saw this after Uri when key Uttar Pradesh state polls were 12 weeks away, and now after Pulwama when the Lok Sabha election is six weeks away. At other times, he has shown a lack of skill to craft a politics which lessens security threats. Kashmir is a perfect example.

When the people of Kashmir are with the government, Pakistan-inspired terrorism finds the going tough. This was seen in the Atal Bihari Vajpayee and the Manmohan Singh years. Sending planes to bomb terrorist camps inside Pakistan won't end terrorist attacks against us. Terrorist outfits are by now entrenched so deep in that country's social and political fabric that the army-controlled Pakistani state finds it expedient to use them rather than eliminate them.

The Wire, 14 March, 2019

Faulty Politics, Intel Failures Led to J&K Ttragedy

Whatever the promised Indian response to Jaish-e-Mohammad's recent fidayeen attack on a CRPF convoy in Kashmir's Pulwama district, which took dozens of lives, it is by now evident that India is not united in dealing with the terrorist outrage. The sincere expressions of solidarity of Congress leader Rahul Gandhi and other top Opposition leaders appear to have been in vain.

Never before has the country been faced with such a shocking state of affairs in dealing with externally-induced terrorism and its foreign patrons. Extreme right wing elements have attacked the properties of Kashmiri people and other Muslims in Jammu, the state's winter capital. Their retaliation is against fellow Indians, not the JeM and Pakistan. And the hyper-active official communications machinery as well as the BJP's social media armies have not bothered to help ordinary people make this crucial distinction. The government and its bailiff in Kashmir, the state's governor Satyapal Malik, are yet to take any meaningful deterrent action against the communal gangs.

The trouble has now spread to other states. At the behest of student and social outfits, which were earlier active in cow vigilantism and 'love jehad' criminalities, hundreds of Kashmiri students in Dehradun and elsewhere have been turned away by their colleges. In reaction, Valley Muslims observed a shut-down on Sunday. In the 1965 and 1971 wars, Kashmiri Muslims had handed over Pakistani infiltrators to the police.

In order to underline the nation's unity at a moment such as this, the government should have actively disseminated the idea that the people of Kashmir were victims of violence, and had nothing to do with the fidayeen attack. The complex politics of Kashmir is not reducible to a Hindu-Muslim binary, as communal Hindus and the Pakistani state seek to do. It does appear that JeM has given communal elements in India the perfect gift as the Lok Sabha elections draw near.

This is the background in which we seek the understanding of other nations in the wake of the Pulwama attack. We are unlikely to be taken at face value. How the Pakistan-China axis responds to an Indian retaliation is an unknown. At a time when the US is negotiating with the Taliban prior to ending its military presence in Afghanistan, Beijing is likely to run its policy close to Islamabad's with an eye to creating leverage for itself in the post-US period there.

As we contemplate recent events, aside from the debilitating crass politics on display, two negatives stand out. The first of these is intelligence failure. The JeM had circulated a video just two days before the strike, indicating that an explosives-laden car would be used to create a major impact, but its meaning was not understood, although in January 2018 too the Jaish had circulated a video before attacking a CRPF training compound in the same broad Awantipora area in Pulwama district. Earlier, in 2016, the CRPF had come under attack on the same road, at Pantha Chowk, not far from Awantipora.

Yet, the intelligence professionals failed to link the latest JeM video to the unduly long CRPF convoy that the government was planning to move up the Jammu-Srinagar highway. They should have.

It would seem the JeM had advance knowledge of CRPF movements and had got ready the explosives and their fidayeen. It had done its homework. But our government had not. The J&K government, under Central rule, was found sleeping on the job.

The second failure concerns the CRPF itself for not considering it grossly unwise to move a convoy of as many as 78 vehicles, ferrying more than 2,500 jawans, in a part of Kashmir which has been a site of encounters on a near daily basis for two and a half years.

Besides, it is evident that existing protocols were not adhered to, and this seems a regular failing with the CRPF. This force seems particularly vulnerable when it moves its jawans, as has also been seen repeatedly in the Naxal-affected parts of Chhatisgarh.

Should politicians placed in top positions readily give a terrorist attack by a Pakistan-based group a religious and a partisan twist? And if they do so, should they not be disciplined? It won't do to single out the Kashmiri separatists alone for admonition, although in the present instance these elements would have been as surprised as anyone else by the strike at the CRPF convoy.

It is to be regretted that a senior Jammu BJP politician, who is a minister of state at the Centre, wore his communal colours on the sleeve by publicly attacking leaders of mainstream parties in the Kashmir Valley for being "apologetic" about terrorists. This travesty of the truth was peddled on the day that the Abdullahs- the father and the son- as well as Mehbooba Mufti had condemned the terrorist action at Pulwama in no uncertain terms.

Unfortunately, J&K governor Satyapal Malik too disregarded his constitutional status- which enjoins on him to remain above the fray- to target mainstream politicians without any reason at a time when the state is under Central rule, the local politicians having been evicted from government in questionable circumstances.

Typically, the security situation in Kashmir is a subset of the political circumstances. It has deteriorated unconscionably over the past four years as the Centre has encouraged anti-Muslim communal politics to gain salience in Kashmir valley.

Even official data presented to Parliament suggests that recruitment by Islamist militant groups (encouraged by Pakistan) has risen five-fold since 2013 (more than 300 teenage and very young adult jihadists being present today as against around 70 earlier). Small wonder that the security forces have had to work overtime.

Official figures suggest that around 250 militants were killed in 2018 alone. This is touted as the efficiency of the Central government. But nowhere does the government say that radicals sprout the minute one is shot down because the politics have gone awry. Nor is the rising curve of fatalities in the forces highlighted. The 20-year old who ploughed his explosives-filled car into the CRPF convoy was by all accounts recruited only a year ago. Before that he had led a mundane life.

Faulty politics, and an adamant refusal on the part of the Centre to engage different elements in the Valley in a coherent conversation aimed at reconciliation and moderation, has eaten away the middle ground in a Muslim-majority region that borders Pakistan. That is India's tragedy.

Its architects are extremist politicians who dare to lecture the country on nationalism and patriotism. They suppress the fact that their brand of politics has led to a bitter harvest. Pathankot, Uri and now Pulwama have occurred over the past few years as dangerous ideologues have been given a free pass.

Abetted by irresponsible sections of the media, this myopic lot today roots for all-out war against Pakistan (and against Kashmiris, and Muslims in general, as the current situation is testimony) without regard for the consequences. To them all Kashmiri Muslims are terrorists and Pakistanis when the opposite is actually the case. Saner voices in politics and the media need to be bolder in their assertion. The politics of hate succeeds only when amplified by a quiescent media.

The Asian Age & The Deccan Chronicle, February 19, 2019

Rahul Alone Gives the BJP Sleepless Nights

"Cometh the hour, cometh the man!" goes the saying (and we may improve it by adding "woman"). With national polls practically at the door, we shall know who the man or the woman is going to be only after the election has flashed past us, not before, such is the tricky electoral wicket. The political scene is riddled with uncertainties.

If the Congress has notched up tide-turning recent victories in states, the BJP has enviable organisational prowess and vast money resources with which to dazzle the voter, browbeat opponents, and win over turncoats, in addition to the crowd-pulling abilities of PM Narendra Modi.

Until a month and a half ago, when the Assembly election results for three key Hindi heartland results came in, it was plausible to give Modi higher probability marks than others for leading the next coalition government at the Centre. But the situation has not remained static.

In order to avoid misconceptions, it is necessary to underline that we are firmly in the coalition universe already. Even the present government is a coalition of several parties, a political khichri, with the BJP leading it. The BJP is unlikely to have won 31 per cent of the national vote in 2014 (and enough Parliament seats to have a majority on its own) if it had fought the polls alone.

Especially given the none-too-bright record of the present regime, few can doubt that the next government too will be a coalition. With its customary shrewdness, BJP's progenitor

RSS recently let out that a hung Parliament was the most likely eventuality in the current situation, puncturing any possible bravado talk on the BJP's part of winning a majority.

The BJP's present attack line that the Opposition parties offer only unstructured chaos is, thus, plain unsubtle propaganda. The point really is which political parties line up on which side of the basic ideological and political dividing line that separates the BJP from the Congress.

Further, all concerned will be keenly watching which leader from the BJP or from the ranks of its rivals is likely to attract the most support in a hung parliament. There are noteworthy probable claimants for the top job on both sides. Their names are a subject of open speculation.

Being the incumbent leader, Modi is, of course, the pre-eminent contender from the BJP-RSS quarters. His capacity to draw attention can never be in doubt. But his government coming up short on delivery in the wake of turbo-charged propaganda at every step, its principal characteristic, has boosted hopes not only among rival parties, but also (with RSS blessings) of some within the saffron camp.

On the other side of the fence, Congress leader Rahul Gandhi has, in the course of two gruelling years, slow-marched his way into the arc of contention—first encircling the countryside, as it were, in line with Chairman Mao's famous dictum. His putative secular camp rivals for the top job after the election—principally West Bengal Chief Minister Mamata Banerjee and BSP leader Mayawati—appear to be more virtual reality than reality.

In fact, what they seem to possess is their derived status (besides their ambition). They will get any traction at all if and only if Rahul Gandhi's Congress either produces more MPs than the BJP does or is just a shade behind the BJP in parliamentary numbers, and not if it falls disappointingly short of a certain threshold.

In short, if the Congress does poorly, the non-Congress secular camp pretenders to the throne that make so much anti-

BJP noise these days will also be ambushed by history. Can distributaries be bigger than the main stream eventually, no matter how much froth they produce?

Gandhi's case is, in fact, an instructive one. His rising stature in public estimation (and acceptability as a political figure of substance) came into full view with the Gujarat Assembly election of 2017 when his party nearly snatched a victory from the entrenched BJP-RSS in the state although it had been a low-impact customer for long, and practically absent from Gujarat's electoral calculus in the preceding two decades.

The Nehru-Gandhi scion was the indefatigable star campaigner for his side. He first united a divided state party and got it battle-ready. He showed *sangfroid* and negotiating skill when he successfully pulled in non-party young firebrands like Hardik Patel, Jignesh Mewani and Alpesh Thakore, whose hallmark was rebellion, to do battle alongside him.

Gandhi also overcame the doubts of a deeply sceptical public. When one recalls that period, it is possible to make the argument that if PM Modi was not a Gujarat native, and if he hadn't pleaded with the voters to come to his aid as he faced an acid test, his party may well have come off second best.

A few months later, it became evident that Gujarat was not a flash in the pan for the Congress leader. His campaigning energy and political strategising stopped a rampaging BJP in Karnataka. Modi and BJP president Amit Shah worked as hard in the Karnataka Assembly election as they had done in Gujarat, but this was of no avail. For them, in Karnataka, the 'home-state effect' was absent.

Later the same year, Chhatisgarh, Madhya Pradesh and Rajasthan (bitterly feuding Congress factions were made to cooperate in these states too) fell to the Congress as the BJP was forced to cede space even in regions of these states where the RSS had been entrenched practically since Independence.

Elections are hard to call, but there seems to be a certain wind blowing that disturbs the equanimity of the ruling dispensation. It is the fast-changing texture of politics which has compelled the government—in an attempt to woo back voters—to allow education and job quotas even for income tax-payers among the Hindu upper caste, and this strikes people as odd.

A government that had set out to bring about economic, social and political reform is obliged to take recourse to old-fashioned reservation policies to pull its chestnuts out of the fire.

It is not confident enough to bank on the premise that while the Congress had notched up Assembly wins, voters do a different arithmetic for Lok Sabha elections. Psephology suggests that in India's case the parliamentary vote tends to go the same way as in an assembly if the voting for the two is within six months of one another. That's an added headache for the BJP, and a plus for Gandhi.

But state polls are history. Now the Congress leader will be sorely tested in two areas. He must do better in UP than his opponents think. Priyanka Gandhi's spectacular induction may be helpful here. Gandhi also needs to bag a couple of pre-poll allies. That'll be a crucial asset in augmenting numbers if the result shows a hung parliament, as is more than likely.

Rahul Gandhi is the lone Opposition leader who has challenged this government and the PM across the board—on issues of economics, politics and ideology, besides the negative impact of government policies on ordinary Indians; other Modi opponents have picked their battles selectively. He is the opponent the BJP fears.

Asian Age & The Deccan Chronicle, January 28, 2019

Priyanka Gandhi is Embarking on a High-Risk Mission in Uttar Pradesh

Priyanka Gandhi Vadra, once seen as a potential bright star of Indian politics, was certainly the most charismatic election campaigner among all Indian politicians—young or old—on view in the late 90s. She was in her 20s but her electioneering caught national attention. They talked about her in the villages and in the towns.

On the stump, Priyanka—affable and spontaneous—was a natural. She was capable of repartee but didn't make long-winded speeches or snide remarks. She strongly resembled her grandmother Indira, and that did it for most people.

There was another thing. Unlike others of the clan—Jawaharlal Nehru downwards—Priyanka speaks mellifluous Hindi, straight out of her native Allahabad, as though she had been born there and never left that eastern UP city.

A few years ago, when a gobsmacked television interviewer asked Priyanka Gandhi where her beautiful Hindi diction and vocabulary came from, she said with ease: "From Mrs. Teji Bachchan, from whom I learnt", referring to the cine superstar Amitabh Bachchan's late mother. That the Gandhis and the Bachchans, once very good friends, had an inexplicable falling out didn't matter to Priyanka.

Even when everything seemed right, Priyanka suddenly disappeared from public view after briefly campaigning in the 2014 Lok Sabha poll. She has hardly been seen in public in the last five years. Theories about her absence abounded. That she was busy raising her kids was, of course, a no-brainer explanation. Two other political 'explanations' in circulation related to darker things.

The more prominent of these was sibling rivalry. If Rahul Gandhi, who lacked natural charisma, had to step into his mother Sonia's shoes, it might be best that Priyanka tucked herself away. It was implied that Rahul would suffer by comparison. Given that Rahul has since earned his spurs, that theory appears to have run out of steam.

The other political 'explanation' was damaging to Priyanka personally. It was said that, by association, she was tainted by her businessman husband Robert Vadra, who appears to be in all sorts of troubles with the authorities on account of his business transactions.

Vadra has dismissed all this as political vendetta by the BJP. But many even in the top tiers of the Congress accepted the stories, and believed that with her husband's reputation dogging her, Priyanka would not return to politics.

The Wednesday decision of Congress president Rahul Gandhi to pitchfork his sister to the forefront of the Lok Sabha poll battle caught everyone by surprise, most of all Congress's Gandhi loyalists. Being made the party's general secretary for eastern UP, which takes in Prime Minister Narendra Modi's constituency of Varanasi, is akin to entering the lion's den. In effect, Priyanka Gandhi is going to be leading the Congress' shock troops. It is unlikely she is doing this against her will.

Suddenly the theories about her five-year absence from politics—from sibling rivalry to Vadra's business deals—don't hold up. By now her brother has made a mark, and Priyanka now has a chance to make hers. Indeed, if reverse psychology is anything, the argument can be made that Priyanka wouldn't have dared take this step if her husband's business deals were irregular.

She knows the lie of the land in UP, and has been a participant in decision-making processes in the Congress at key junctures.

It was she who finally swung the Congress-Samajwadi

Party alliance for the UP assembly election in early 2017 by personally prevailing on Akhilesh Yadav to part with 100 seats. In hindsight, the alliance was a conceptual disaster. The upper caste voters deserted the Congress the minute it allied with the SP.

When Rahul Gandhi was made vice-president of the Congress and Sonia Gandhi was away for treatment in the US, Priyanka became her brother's advisor and political confidante, sitting in on strategy sessions with him, presumably at his request, dealing with state leaders, especially those from UP.

Now that she will be a Congress general secretary for the more tricky part of UP for the party in the run-up to the Lok Sabha election, Priyanka will have to re-do her electoral and political math in light of the humiliating defeat suffered (by the Congress and the SP) at the hands of the BJP in the last state poll. So, it is a high-risk game that she is embarking on, a kamikaze mission almost.

If Congress performs creditably, Priyanka may be in politics for the long haul. If the results go the other way, she will probably have to withdraw in ignominy. For dynasts, the room for error is limited. Priyanka has already been cut some slack and offered her present post after the last UP assembly poll drubbing.

Rahul envisages for his sister, and for Jyotiraditya Scindia, given the position of general secretary for western UP, a significant role that goes much beyond state supervision in the Lok Sabha poll. Priyanka and Jyotiraditya have been entrusted with the responsibility of reviving the Congress in this crucial state. On Priyanka rests the burden of expectations.

If she succeeds, she will be catapulted to the top of the decision-making hierarchy alongside her brother. This could catalyse changes in the Congress organisation. Success could also push Jyotiraditya to the top.

In the past, Priyanka has shown she has traction with the people. In 1999, some may recall, Arun Nehru, a cousin of Priyanka's father, the late Prime Minister Rajiv Gandhi, was contesting the Lok Sabha election from Rae Bareli, which was once Indira Gandhi's parliamentary seat, on the BJP ticket, after parting with the Congress on a bitter note.

Priyanka addressed just one meeting there. She said to the crowds, "Don't you know this man stabbed my father in the back? I am surprised you are even entertaining him here!" And that was the end of the late Arun Nehru's parliamentary career. Initially, he had appeared to be coasting along smoothly, but Priyanka's quick-fire intervention sent him crashing.

If Priyanka manages to revive the Congress magic of the past, it would spell trouble for the BJP. The Yogi-Modi combination has made a mess of things in UP and dissatisfaction is said to be high. This gives Priyanka a toe hold. Failure to leverage the dissatisfaction would mean exile for the Congress.

Dynastic placements are hardly something to pray for in a democracy. But when dynasts of their own volition lead the front against attempts to impose a religion-based majoritarian order, the enterprise they are engaged in has the effect of transforming their politics. In the end, it is the values they champion that matter.

The Wire, January 24, 2019

Modi Government's Paranoia Laid Bare Before Parliamentary Polls

When Narendra Modi, the challenger, campaigned with sensational vigour in 2013 and the early part of 2014 for the Lok Sabha election in May that year, he said he had a dream of a New India—where farmers' incomes would double and employment for the youth will be aplenty—to beckon.

Five years on, that spirit is pre-history. There is disenchantment and despair among the owning classes; the toilers have a sense of being sold short. Those in between—the middle classes, who were praised sky high by the prime minister in his New Year's day interview to a news agency—have been squeezed by joblessness, no tax relief, and petrol rates crashing every price barrier much of the time.

Faith in the regime's promises has grown scarce. This is the real change from 2014. In order to remain in the hunt, Modi seeks to use an imagined past—his five years in office—as a crutch to traverse the treacherous terrain of the present since there is no brave new world to credibly project as the country slips into election mode for the Lok Sabha polls in May.

The Prime Minister misses the irony of his words when he still promises a "*majboot*" or strong government, as he did at his party's national convention in New Delhi last Saturday.

But the going is tough. These years have been inglorious. No set of five consecutive years since 1947 has been as flawed—and this country has known famine, war, defeat, times of unsettled political authority, and a suspension of liberties as during the Emergency.

This makes Modi's strategy of pumping up the past seem uncaring, and probably self-defeating. But the prime minister appears to be doing just that. In his January 1 interview, he maintained that his demonetisation policy (which was strictly his own, with even the finance minister being cut out of the consultations) and implementing the GST the way his government planned it, was necessary and effective and successful.

This is akin to sprinkling salt in the wounds of the most devastated sections of the country.

The boldest move to emanate—in the closing weeks of the regime—from the most influential office in the land is last week's offer of a 10% reservation in jobs and higher education to high caste Hindus if their family earnings are less than Rs 65,000 a month. This brings people rich enough to pay income tax into the quota tent, creates yet another creamy layer, effectively sealing the fate of the genuine poor among the upper caste.

Even BJP MPs worry what reaction their constituents might confront them with in respect of what sycophants and time-servers have called a "game-changer".

Reserving 10% jobs for the poor among the upper castes is not a new idea. It is a failed old idea. It had been attempted by prime minister P.V. Narasimha Rao in 1997 in the wake of the backlash to prime minister V.P. Singh's Mandal policy. The move had been struck down by the Supreme Court for being unmindful of the basic structure of the constitution. And yet the Modi government has played the same card, in full knowledge of the history.

Doesn't that make it an election-time sleight of hand, a "*chunavi jumla*", to recall BJP chief Amit Shah's counter-famous words about a reckless promise made by Modi to voters in 2014 that was impossible to fulfil?

If this is how the new year and the BJP's new election campaign have begun, the saffron party may be called upon to rue its future at leisure should history repeat itself as a tragedy, to quote Marx's famous words of warning.

Great nations can survive policy failures and broken promises. It's much harder to repair social cohesion and the nation's unity when these have been ruptured as a conscious act by the constellation of forces that emerged with the rise of Modi to power, and were permitted to conduct themselves with a rare latitude and impunity.

The cow-related violence was nothing but that. Every act of communal conflagration promoted under the RSS-BJP dispensation points in the same direction. The latest example of causing social upheaval by fiat is the push to amend the Citizenship Act in order to bring aliens into the country on the sole basis of religion. All of Northeastern India has risen in revolt as a result, in likely electoral terms hurting the BJP more than any other party.

A towering Assam intellectual and Cambridge scholar, the 80-year old Hiren Gohain, who has been honoured with the Sahitya Akademi award, has had the charge of sedition pressed against him by the BJP government for opposing the Citizenship (Amendment) Bill at a public meeting.

In today's climate anyone can be hounded as an "anti-national", and a collaborator of Pakistan out to defeat the present regime.

The regime is in paranoia. A remarkable thing about each of Modi's five years in office—apart from policies that proved to be sordid failures—was the propensity of the leadership to attack and demonise a party that was not in power.

This did not stop the Congress from snatching victory from the BJP in the three Hindi heartland states last month. But the BJP is undeterred. After the tactic so emphatically failed, Modi continues to believe that an unceasing attack on the nationally out-of-power Congress is the only weapon of defence in the BJP's depleting arsenal. Ordinary Indians are aghast at the current goings-on, which seemed bad enough before news about the Rafale-related corruption charge broke.

If the BJP's political allies of decades are deserting it as the Lok Sabha election looms, presenting a picture which is in such stark contrast with 2014, it is because they have sensed the public mood.

And they are not the only ones. The RSS has too. It can be inferred that the mother-body of all Hindutva outfits has permitted the speculation to grow that Union minister Nitin Gadkari could be a likely contender for Prime Minister, should the BJP have the opportunity to again lead a coalition. And, in an open letter to the RSS, Sanghpriya Gautam, an 80-year old founder-member of the BJP from Uttar Pradesh, has endorsed the idea of replacing party president Amit Shah as well.

These strange twists before the next battle for India is joined suggest the spread of disarray in the saffron establishment.

The Wire, January 17, 2019

Handling Politics When the Breeze is Changing

When the BJP was expecting to steamroll the Congress, it went for a six over mid-wicket. This alters not just the political lie of the land but national political dynamics as well as we approach the Lok Sabha elections.

Suddenly, the expectation has been given birth in the minds of the people—not just the political class—that a credible challenge to the Modi-Shah BJP has sprouted.

There is a sense of loosening up in the country—a feeling of normal breathing, a dispelling of the suffocation produced by the overt and persistent majoritarian actions of the Sangh Parivar elements which appeared to enjoy the indulgence of those who matter.

What form the riposte of the Opposition parties will assume in different states is all lively speculation now. The conceptual confusions that attended the very mention of the prospect of multiple parties combining to challenge the supposed masters of the game are dissolving.

The "hesitations of history" imposed on Congress leader Rahul Gandhi by the circumstances of his birth and by Narendra Modi's unremitting demonising of Prime Ministers Jawaharlal Nehru, and Indira and Rajiv Gandhi—magnified by leading media sections that praised even questionable moves of those in power—appear to have melted away.

The current Congress leader has demonstrably shaken off his fetters. Observers now note Gandhi's maturity, his gentleness (which stands out in such sharp contrast with the boorishness of many of his Sangh Parivar opponents), and his soft humour. These set him apart from his adversaries who had made the spewing of venom against political opponents routine.

Gandhi has now even demonstrated that he is Prime Minister Modi's equal in terms of what psephologists call the "strike rate". If the BJP won 55 seats where Modi campaigned in the recent elections, Gandhi's tally was 50—not much to choose there. This hardly used to be the case earlier.

After providing evidence of grit on the campaign trail and political savvy in managing edgy Congress factions, the bane of the party, especially at election time, the Congress president should forgo the appellation "chor" or thief when speaking of the self-appointed "chowkidar"—the guard of the premises—of the nation. More restrained language will do our democracy a world of good.

Stooping low to emulate the leading lights of the BJP was never advisable. After the Congress' major wins in a head-to-head contest with the BJP, this is now not even necessary in order to impress the "shirtless" who may incline to rough speech to show machismo—the path favoured by the Hindu nationalists in recent times as they worked to mobilise large sections of society.

While it is true that those in power today (and some others) had reviled Gandhi's father in the same language, paying back in kind in such matters is not the civilised way, even if men like Donald Trump (and others) do this all the time. False delineations of words and actions of political opponents, a stock-in- trade of important ruling party politicians, is also a temptation best avoided.

It has become evident that the ruling party's defeat in the recent state polls in three Hindi heartland states, which had played a vital part in the BJP's famous win in the parliament election of 2014, is attributable not so much to the functioning of the ruling party as to its leading demagogue and ideologue of the past five years.

More than the PM's style of campaigning (galling though his reference to Sonia Gandhi as the "vidhwa" or widow was), analysts of different shades are united in the view that rural distress was at the core of voter disenchantment. Allied to this crucial cause was the faltering unemployment data for nearly a five-year period, which was seen as Modi reneging on a key promise.

The crisis in agriculture and falling unemployment were both fed by the demonetisation policy of 2016, a policy that Modi had personally driven with single-minded devotion, cutting out all others in the political executive, and key advisers.

Thus, barring the gainfully employed sections that form the backbone of the urban middle class, practically all sections of society had begun to nurse a grievance against the economic policies of the Modi government. This is a picture that was on view across Madhya Pradesh, Chhattisgarh and Rajasthan.

Madhya Pradesh under Shivraj Singh Chouhan's leadership appeared to resist the trend, but the psychological disequilibrium triggered in the lives of ordinary people by the policies of the Centre defined for Indians in a basic way the main motif of the recent assembly elections.

Will the graph of the state elections be valid for the Lok Sabha poll? Aren't issues debated at the Assembly level different from those raised in Lok Sabha elections? Analysis of polling data over time suggests that, generally, if the national election is held within about six months of assembly polls, then the trend seen at the state level only intensifies in the Lok Sabha elections. And we saw in the recent elections that the key deciding factors were the Centre's harmful policies, rather than those of the three BJP-run state governments. Logically, this should continue to be valid in the parliament election early next year.

Until recently, the RSS-BJP were seen as running the most fearsome election fighting machine in the world, which was at it round the clock, even when there were no elections. The polls in the Hindi-speaking states, which were the RSS-BJP's special area of influence, have shown this to be a myth. The propaganda of invincibility was circulated by the RSS itself with the help of friendly sections of the media, some of whom even expanded this pedestrian hypothesis into a shaky theory in quickie books.

It was noteworthy in the Madhya Pradesh election that the BJP was bested by the Congress even in the state's Malwa belt, where deep RSS influence has carried from even before Independence. For the main Opposition party, this reveals a favourable juncture. But there is nothing automatic in life or politics. Rahul Gandhi and his party have laid the groundwork. They need to show the skill and the wisdom to take forward the momentum. The BJP, the party in power, is hardly expected to be sitting on its haunches.

Asian Age & The Deccan Chronicle, December 17, 2018

Turning Back the Clock in India's Politics

We are in the middle of elections to five state assemblies, whose outcome will be no less than a landmark in our political life. Undue notice may not have been taken of these polls if the ruling BJP were not seen to be on trial in three of the five states.

These three have been the BJP's comfort zone for long, and in recent years have been turned into a Hindutva playground, showcasing—along with UP and Gujarat—the party's understanding of the so-called Hindu way of life and of rule by Hindus (rather than by elected citizens whose religious identity is not underlined), while giving no more than a formal nod to the Constitution, a remarkable document which emphasises pluralism for a country of bewildering diversity.

These particular states are a microcosm of Prime Minister Narendra Modi and his party's conception of Bharat. Naturally then, as regards these elections, there is also a deep national curiosity- and for many anxiety- about whether the Congress, the country's oldest party with a very different register of politics and ideology from the BJP's, can present itself as an adequate challenger to BJP's approach to politics and life, and appear as a substitute for it in the public eye.

Outright wins and losses in Rajasthan, Madhya Pradesh and Chhatisgarh will of course be a leading marker of the direction public life takes as we look ahead. But clear victories/ defeats are not an essential requirement. Even if the BJP or the Congress do not lose emphatically, which means one of them remains a somewhat equal force even in defeat, the prospect of a continuing contest between two distinct brands of politics will remain alive in the future.

This will matter early next year when the country will be thrown into the whirlwind of preparations for the Lok Sabha election of 2019. There the canvas will be the whole country and the results will provide a clearer idea of the kind of country Indians want.

Do we as a nation seek the same kind of politics as we did in 2014 in the sense of giving the saffron party a no-holds-barred control of our polity and the governing structures, unlike, say, in the time of Vajpayee, when the BJP had to remain content with being constrained by its secular allies?

Alongside this had come the overthrow of the Congress lock, stock and barrel- indicating that the country felt the need to try out a different party on a full sway basis (as was the case up to the 1970s with the Congress). Fatigue with the Congress was evident as was evident the urge and temptation to try out the Modi brand of leader, not just the saffron party.

Modi and Shah naturally took this to be a deep-going endorsement of their leadership and long-term commitment to the saffron party by the people of India. The BJP president recently declared that his party was going to rule India for the next fifty years, which some saw as a threat to not relinquish power- leaving no stone unturned to remain in the saddle.

But perhaps this was no more than carefree exuberance on the part of the BJP leader. The reality on the ground, as crucial elections approach, cannot however give him and the Prime Minister the comfort they seek from the national mood.

After all, no promise of note made in 2014 by Modi to the electorate has been met. The economy is in poor shape. Unemployment is running high. BJP's allies have turned uncertain. The Gujarat state election was barely won last year. Karnataka this year was lost. A string of by-elections in several states have produced a gloomy verdict.

So, the party appears to have taken precautions, and pointedly changed direction to overlook the "*sabka saath, sabka vikas*" mantra which became such a vote-catcher in 2014, the slogan that was emblematic of the election which brought the BJP to power in a landslide, giving history a turn.

For the past couple of months, in the run-up to the crucial state polls and as preparation for next year's national election, the idea being repeatedly dinned into the public by the BJP, RSS, and its militant affiliates, is related to the construction of the proposed Ram Temple in Ayodhya, alongside barely camouflaged appeals to violate the recent order of the Supreme Court permitting women of menstrual age to enter the Sabrimala shrine in Kerala. This is surprising for a party holding office.

After 1989, when the BJP first began to aggressively raise the question of the Ram Mandir and finally in December 1992 succeeded in demolishing the Babri Masjid, it was the challenger in Indian politics. The Congress hegemony had been dealt a blow by the desertion of V.P.Singh, and the BJP seized the chance to mount its own offensive on the subject of the temple at Ayodhya. This was BJP's way to legitimise its communal assault.

Much happened in the period before 2014 when Mody rode to power, keeping communalism in the backdrop and front-loading issues of day-to-day survival of the common people in order to attract greater traction as the party that aimed to supplant the Congress as the national icon of politics.

But the bid seems to be coming unstuck. Evidently, the BJP never did change its strategic vision. In 2014, it now seems, it had only made a tactical retreat in speaking of the all-round development of all.

The saffron party, now as the party in power with the largest parliamentary majority in a quarter century, is obliged to hark back to its slogan of a quarter century ago, throwing caution to the wind. This is a time when it should have been blowing the trumpet on the strength of its achievements. That is not the case, however.

Perhaps the ruling party is only too aware of its

unwholesome record in office- on the economic and the social front. The clock is being turned back on the political front, with Ayodhya hitting the headlines again.

We can't know what this means for the elections ahead. But it is noticeable that paeans of praise to the political hero of 2014 are muted in the BJP-ruled states going to the polls, with party's state leaders being highlighted instead in Rajasthan, MP and Chhatisgarh. Perhaps we are at a cusp in politics.

Asian Age & The Deccan Chronicle, November 19, 2018

Rahul Gandhi Must Forge a Different Congress

If Narendra Modi had set the tone in late 2013 and early 2014 by unleashing a no-holds-barred attack on Sonia and Rahul Gandhi, thus inaugurating an era of personalised name-calling in politics in which every FIR (First Information Report lodged with the police) led to Jawaharlal Nehru, months before crucial state elections, Gandhi appears to have taken aim squarely at the Prime Minister, with the available material on the Rafale deal and the government struggling with explanations on economic fugitives like Vijay Mallya.

It is clear the Congress chief is seeking to play the conscious catalyser in a likely process of crucial adjustments to the current political equilibrium in the country, depending on the outcome in the upcoming Assembly elections, which lead on to the next Lok Sabha poll.

The deep-going Rafale-related suspicions of wrongdoing can be immediately stanched if the government agreed to a probe by a Joint Parliamentary Committee. It strains logic that it should reject the idea of probe—whose announcement can be in its self-interest—into suspected malfeasance involving Rs 59,000 crores of taxpayers' money.

To top these murky goings-on is the sharp deterioration in the security climate in Kashmir, which do India no credit. After the beheading of a BSF soldier on the LoC, the Army Chief has called for a retaliatory strategy. But his words undercut defence minister Nirmala Sitharaman, who just days earlier airily informed a friendly Hindi television station that the Indians were severing the heads of the Pakistanis but were not prone to "display"—a kind of reverse of the so-called surgical strike strategy.

In the national interest, all of this, besides the hardships on the economic front, would naturally lead the Opposition to ask questions of the government. These may also be a factor in the forthcoming state elections. However, the overall advantage may still be presumed to lie with the ruling party and government as it has the state machinery at its beck and call.

The State can go at express speed on a propaganda blitz with the aid of the bludgeoned sections of the media, although the latter's ability to lead the narrative is waning. Still, the regime's opponents cannot match its propaganda resources.

With enormous punitive powers at its command, the government can also arm-twist certain types of opponents into submission. This too is an advantage only the ruling party at the Centre has when it turns its back on ethics.

BSP (Bahujan Samaj Party) heroine Mayawati's falter in joining an anti-BJP coalition of Opposition parties in key north Indian states, after holding out such a promise, may be cited as an example of the government's abilities in the dark arts.

Assembly polls in Rajasthan, Madhya Pradesh, Chhattisgarh and Mizoram are barely eight weeks away, and in Telangana perhaps less. In light of Mayawati's reported moves, the Congress Party has already suffered a jolt. Can the Opposition's hopes be revived? Gandhi must step into the breach with an on-the-ground dynamism that he had shown in Gujarat and Karnataka.

In those states Gandhi gave the impression of taking on the heavy lifting himself, cutting through state factions, working on possible brackets of cooperation with various political entities, and taking an active and visible interest in settling intra-party rivalries. He also seemed unafraid of the criticism of not showing sufficient patience with certain parties and groups. This overall approach paid dividend.

In the case of Madhya Pradesh and Chhattisgarh, however, the Congress stance appears to have been tentative, one born of insecurity, leading to an accent on trying overmuch to please the BSP for fear of losing out to the BJP if an alliance with the dalit party did not come through.

Mayawati, in contrast, showed panache. In Chhattisgarh, she secretly roped in Ajit Jogi while the Congress waited on her. The whole episode suggests that the BSP leader has decided not to be with the principal opponents of the regime in any state, including Uttar Pradesh.

In the circumstances, Mayawati's interlocutors, especially the Congress, can only survive by displaying boldness, which since Indira Gandhi has not been the party's dominant characteristic. This calls for a barnstorming mindset—to campaign vigorously with the dalit communities, for whose youth the BJP has been an object of anger in recent times.

Mayawati is losing sight of the fact that young dalits, in UP especially, had gone to the BJP in droves in 2014, and not to her, and this time around they might be looking for a third option in case she pitched in with the BJP.

In a scenario of this kind, attempting the Hardik Patel-Jignesh Mevani coordinate adopted last year in Gujarat suggests itself. These young, radical politicians of different persuasions had borne an unusual political responsibility by going against set patterns and had paired with the Congress.

Such young politicians need to be unearthed in the northern part of the country as well. The reliance on compromised politicians in general, including within the Congress, when taking on entrenched communal tendencies, can hardly be overstated.

In a quarter century, for various reasons, the Congress has not been the preferred destination of the youth, who now seem to have gone off on communal or caste tangents in the main, with the communal call being the louder. This, however, brought them nothing but misery.

Narrow identity-based ideologies rooted in the far right

are known to produce economic despair, especially for the middle and the poor classes, and bring about deep social cleavages and insecurities. This was the scenario in which Gujarat had made a move toward the Congress last year.

In Gujarat, for the youth, the Congress was the only probable alternative; and two, it had a new, energetic, young leader in Gandhi who looks sincere, if too earnest, and appears not corrupt. The latter was decidedly a factor. Earlier the Congress has been a probable alternative but without making a difference.

When Modi and Gandhi are now head-to-head, the former is not an automatic choice any more. That's been clear for some time, as recent polling data also attests. With the country's woes mounting, and despair seizing the youth, this is not an unnatural outcome. But the Congress, especially, must remember it is starting with a very narrow base. Regime criticism alone cannot do the trick. Creative collaborations are vital.

Rajasthan, Madhya Pradesh and Chhattisgarh, in each of which the RSS-BJP are in power, the Congress can only make headway if it shows tactical innovativeness and awareness, and pitches its appeal across all sections, not least because all have borne the brunt, although some more than others. In this terrain lies the Congress' real challenge.

Asian Age & The Deccan Chronicle, September 24, 2018

Silence and Mayhem Cannot Go Together

There is perhaps nothing more striking about Prime Minister Narendra Modi's present tenure—which ends in a few months—than its silence on matters where the clear choice of right and wrong, moral versus immoral, ethics or the want of it, and adherence to the Constitution or its negation, has presented itself.

Since a clear endorsement of what society considers bad, wrong, undesirable or lacking in constitutional propriety or probity cannot be a public good, and may cost at election time, remaining quiet is designed as a clever tactic. Its purpose is to offer comfort to wrongdoers (sometimes evildoers) and suspected criminals, thus causing injury to the notion of what's right, valid and appropriate conduct for an elected government.

That, in turn, amounts to a violation of the compact between the government and the country's citizens, and causes visible injury to the oath every minister of the government takes at the time of being sworn in.

In the process the state and the government lose their authority. The emperor begins to be seen as being denuded. There may be murmurs of rebellion but the people do not rise in revolt because too much force is ranged on the other side. They would rather bide their time.

Two recent instances come to mind—though several more can be cited—of the regime's sly silence. Consider first the case of M.J. Akbar in relation to the vigorous #MeToo campaign and the stunning allegations of sexual predation made against him by more than 20 women. The minister of state for external affairs was eventually forced to resign under the weight of his omissions and commissions in the course of dealing with young women over whom he had authority.

But the point here is the reaction of the BJP, the ruling party; of the RSS, which holds that party's moral compass and is its moral arbiter; and more importantly of the government, especially Prime Minister Narendra Modi, who made Mr Akbar minister, and also external affairs minister Sushma Swaraj under whom he served.

It would be understandable if all the above had remained circumspect and quiet when the minister was overseas on assignment. But BJP and RSS spokesmen, speaking on television, were anything but discreet. They in fact went out of their way to attack the women who had accused Akbar—asking for proof of allegations of sexual misconduct as if these can ever exist (by the very nature of the alleged crime)—and the RSS representatives, in particular, maintaining that India "is not a banana republic and the rule of law exists here".

In effect, the victims of the minister's alleged predatory conduct were sought to be demonised and traduced. Those engaging in this sport gave no evidence of appreciating that moral uprightness is a requirement in governance, not legal proof, when confronted with allegations of wrongdoing.

They had obviously not heard of a former Prime Minister, a man called Lal Bahadur Shastri (who had resigned as railway minister in the Nehru Cabinet, accepting constructive responsibility when a train accident occurred). This may be the RSS' idea of morality, but the Narendra Modi government should have had its own mind on the matter since, unlike the RSS, the government is a creature of the Constitution.

The Prime Minister was morally duty-bound to give the minister marching orders upon his return to India if only to make the point that a sustained record of alleged crimes against women cannot be tolerated as it robs the government as well as the society of its dignity, and the entire class of women of their very being and soul.

But Modi maintained a sphinx-like silence as is his wont, and this encouraged Akbar to file a case of criminal defamation—pointedly not civil defamation—against the first woman to have raised her finger. The government's ear-splitting silence was consistent with its lack of any communication with the public whenever serious crimes against women rocked the country, signifying that the Union government had no sympathy for the females whose bodily integrity had been criminally encroached upon.

Two shameful episodes illustrate this—the Kathua gangrape and murder of an eight-year-old child near Jammu and the subsequent open public defence of the criminals by ministers of the J&K government to the shock of the entire country, with the government at the Centre remaining stoical.

The second numbing episode is that of a BJP MLA in Uttar Pradesh, Kuldeep Singh Sengar, raping a minor girl and having her father tortured and murdered at a police station when he went there to lodge a complaint.

One more recent instance of governmental encouragement through the use of silence as tactic concerns RSS supremo Mohan Bhagwat. During his recent three-day outreach programme in New Delhi, the RSS leader declared, in effect, that while the Supreme Court may be adjudicating the Ayodhya title dispute, in reality it was the Temple Construction Committee (of the Hindutva outfits) that would decide the construction of the Ram temple (at the site where the Babri mosque was felled in 1992)—irrespective of the outcome of the court's labours.

This was nothing if not heaping humiliation on the highest court of the land. But the government just stood and watched in a neutral stance. Perhaps the regime's thinking is in harmony with the outrageous proposition outlined by the top boss of a dangerous outfit whose mention comes up in "Riot after Riot" (to recall the title of a book authored by Akbar in his pre-BJP days).

This is not the only serious infraction the RSS leader is guilty of. Just weeks afterward, delivering his Vijayadashami address on October 18, Bhagwat referred to the permitting of the entry of women to the Sabarimala temple (by a recent order of the Supreme Court) in inflammatory and prejudicial terms, choosing to renew his assault on the top court with an emotional pitch to the target audience, doubtless with a view to rabble-rousing.

In the context of the Sabarimala judgment, the man actually said that "repeated and brazen onslaughts" happened to "Hindu society alone". In a Hindu-majority country, this is a call to arms for the Hindus on a false and hypocritical premise.

The call to arms is not against the Supreme Court, not even only against the traditionally targeted minorities, but on the Constitution itself. Once again, the government answered the challenge with silence.

It is time to ponder if the leader of the RSS would have thought it prudent to speak in this manner and idiom if he didn't have under his command a trained paramilitary style volunteer force, which receives the benign attention of the government. It's also worth wondering what's left of the sheen of the government and the majesty of the law. Big trouble lies ahead. We may as well brace for it.

Asian Age & The Deccan Chronicle, October 22, 2018

Trust Vote Victory for BJP Has Also Brought Alliance Woes to the Fore

The vote on the no-confidence motion debate in the Lok Sabha on Friday, which the Bharatiya Janata Party-led government expectedly won, has turned out to be a revelation.

The Shiv Sena at last came good on its threats to the BJP of walking its own path. Its MPs simply didn't show up in the Lok Sabha on Friday. As a member of the BJP-led NDA coalition, and with representation in the council of ministers at the Centre and in the BJP-led Maharashtra government, it was incumbent upon it to vote against the motion moved by the Modi government's political opponents.

It did nothing of the kind. Indeed, *Saamna,* the Sena mouthpiece, appeared brutal in its declaration on Friday that it won't go with the "Modi dictatorship".

So where does the BJP go from here? Will it sack Udhav Thackeray's ministers in New Delhi and in Mumbai? Will it make moves to topple the Shiv Sena from the leadership of the Bombay Municipal Corporation? On the whole, what shape will the Sena-BJP fight take here on?

If the gloves are off between the Shiv Sena and the BJP as the next Lok Sabha election approaches, can the Sena play for tactical accommodation with the Congress, NCP, or both? Promiscuous conduct has been known to be the stuff of Indian politics. On the other hand, if the BJP sues for peace, to what extent will it go to appease the Sena?

The Shiv Sena, Telugu Desam Party and Akali Dal have been the BJP's nearest allies for decades. Now only the Akalis remain and they too have a plateful of grievances relating to agriculture and to the BJP's muscle-play. As regards the no-trust motion, the Akali Dal position was that it was in sympathy with the TDP's demand—which was the reason why N. Chandrababu Naidu's party brought the no-confidence motion—for a special finance package for Andhra Pradesh.

Besides its principal NDA allies, the BJP has broadly been in tune with the politics of the AIADMK in Tamil Nadu, Odisha's Biju Janata Dal, and the Telangana Rashtra Samiti of KCR. Indeed, the BJP is thought to have shaped some of the AIADMK's postures since the death of J. Jayalalithaa.

Of these parties, the large block of 37 AIADMK MPs eventually voted with the Modi government. Otherwise, the government's score would have dropped to 288. But in the run-up to the vote, through the 12-hours of parliamentary drama as the motion was debated, speculation was rife that the AIADMK was divided. Evidently, several MPs were not comfortable voting with the government, given the state of general dissatisfaction in the country. Willy-nilly, instructions "from above" were finally accepted.

The TRS speech on the motion couldn't have given the BJP much comfort, but the party's MPs walked out of the House before the vote was taken. It is not clear how this should be construed. Was this an indirect favour to the government, in terms of lessening the numbers of those present and voting so that the government count becomes comfortable? But such a reading has greater validity when the call is expected to be tight—when the strength of the government's opponents is nearly as much as that of the treasury benches. This was clearly not the case.

The behaviour of the BJD presents a similar picture. But this party's MPs did not take part in the debate at all. Before the discussion commenced, its leaders announced to the Speaker that they were leaving as they were neither with the BJP nor the Congress.

The catch here is that the motion had not been moved

by the Congress but by the TDP. In reality, perhaps, the BJD did not wish to annoy the government as some of its leading lights are allegedly involved with the chit funds scandal and the party might have calculated it was better to play safe.

On the other hand, party clearly didn't wish to vote with the government. This is both on account of the government's declining—or plateauing—graph in the country and the fact that in Odisha the BJD and the BJP will be pitted against one another in the 2019 elections to both the Lok Sabha and the state assembly.

Participating in the debate, Prime Minister Narendra Modi appeared to insult the two regional parties of Andhra Pradesh—the TDP, not any more an ally, for bringing the no-trust motion, and the YSR Congress, for having "laid a trap" in which the TDP fell. It is to be seen at election time if it has viable allies in this southern state.

Looking at the picture, overall, it would seem that the BJP, quite unlike 2014, does not have willing and eager allies in the southern part of the country, or in the east. Those who are with them, like the AIADMK, are not on the strongest of wickets themselves.

The picture in the north of the country seems less gloomy, although in UP only very minor allies, like the Apna Dal, may be receptive to the saffron party's advances. In Punjab, of course, the Akali Dal and the BJP cannot do without each other. Both will fall to the Congress if they don't pool energies.

Another revelation the no-confidence motion vote threw up was that the BJP was unable to poach MPs from its avowed opponents. It also appeared that there was floor coordination, including at some level even between the Congress and the TDP—parties that have confronted each other over a long period of time. A high-level Congress functionary, who followed the debate cannily, seemed central to this effort.

There appeared initial thinking in the opposition camp that rather than face certain defeat, the parties ranged against the government should walk out protesting loudly as Modi took the floor. Neither TDP nor Congress favoured this line, but their reasons were different.

For the TDP, with the audience back home in mind, the need of the hour was to fight the BJP tooth and nail on account of denial of a special financial package. Its Guntur MP, Jayadev Galla, who led the charge as the first speaker—a rare honour given by a political party to a first-term member—noted without mincing words, "This is Modi regime versus the people of Andhra Pradesh!"

But the reason the Congress was keen on a vote taking place was that it desired the Shiv Sena's conduct on the question of voting with the BJP to be made absolutely clear.

Two important leaders of the political spectrum were also on conscious display. Congress chief Rahul Gandhi, for once ticked all the boxes in the lengthy speech he made. His language, for once, was well considered, and the Hindi delivery fluent. Gandhi spoke without notes and touched on all the crucial issues. But he would no doubt wonder the morning after if it was necessary for him to go and hug Modi after his combative speech, which was appreciated even by political opponents. Do such acts take away from a sense of gravitas?

Prime Minister Modi, as expected, targeted only the Congress, not any other party, and went all out trying to hit out at Rahul and Sonia Gandhi. It was clear who the BJP's real adversaries are on the political- and ideological- landscape. He spoke for 90 minutes but couldn't quite get into his political stride. He got caught in the thicket of statistics and official data, some of it jaded from overuse. This appeared to enthuse no one, not even the BJP benches, though they did applaud dutifully from time to time.

"Janab aankron mein phans gaye!" (the gent was trapped and threw numbers at the people) was the refrain heard afterward, so starkly a reminder of the time of the late P. V. Narasimha Rao. The brooding scholar-intellectual former PM, who everyone thought was devilishly adept in the affairs of

state, had run a minority government quite successfully for a full five-year term, but his time in office saw the ignominy of the demolition of the Babri mosque. This had denuded him of political as well as ideological legitimacy, rendering the Congress a body blow, as he took recourse to a jumble of data to broadcast his government's achievements.

In the election campaign that would be his last, PV, as he was widely known, addressed practically empty grounds where he tried to hide behind *"aankrey"*—data from files meant to highlight his government's achievements (of which there were doubtless many). But no one was interested. Legitimacy had taken flight.

The Wire, July 22, 2018

No-Confidence Vote Will Show if Modi's Camp Still Holds the Aces

The voting on the no-confidence motion on Friday should hold few surprises. The NDA has 314 seats, with the Lok Sabha's current strength being 535. The BJP on its own should be comfortably off with its 273 MPs in the House, the number needed if the House was at its full strength of 543. And yet, the day could be tantalising.

This is on account of two sets of factors—one pertaining to the cohesion within NDA/BJP, and the other relating to not just the possibility of early Lok Sabha polls but these polls being combined with eight Assembly elections, not merely the four that are naturally due this winter (November/December).

In the event the BJP pulls down the Bihar government like it did the J&K, as is being speculated in political circles, this important Hindi-belt state (which yielded the BJP handsome results the last time round) could also be added to the list of states where early polls are no more unthinkable on a balance of possibility turning into a balance of probability.

In a Wire article earlier this year (February 18), this writer had first dwelt on Prime Minister Modi's compulsions that could cause him to move in the direction of an early election, a theme subsequently taken up by many. One of these was that if its performance is below par in Rajasthan, Madhya Pradesh and Chhattisgarh this winter, the BJP will have to go into the April-May 2019 Lok Sabha poll with an electoral setback, and that would hardly be clever.

This especial factor has now been compounded with

government failures being magnified in many more fields (in addition to farm distress, unemployment and the disastrous effects of demonetisation and wayward GST implementation), in particular internal security (Kashmir), foreign affairs and shoddy state of defence preparedness in relation to the military consolidation of the Chinese behemoth in Tibet. No matter where one looks, a pin is down.

In this backdrop, the broad calculation in the ruling camp is said to be shaping in the direction of holding Lok Sabha polls with a fairly large number of state polls. This also ties in with BJP's widely advertised idea of holding Assembly and parliament polls simultaneously, which the Prime Minister has also spoken of.

Given Modi's felicity with indecorous speech and unbecoming aggression when it comes to opponents, the saffron side would anticipate the PM's presence will galvanise the BJP's assembly election prospects also if polls are held at the same time as the Lok Sabha.

Thus, along with state elections in Rajasthan, MP, Chhattisgarh and Mizoram, expected in November/December this year, polls could be held in Andhra Pradesh and Odisha (all due in the early part of 2019), in addition to J&K, where an ally has been toppled, and Bihar, where an ally could be toppled.

That would make a handsome tally of eight states. Will the BJP chance its arm in Maharashtra as well, still banking on Modi being a larger-than-life presence? That seems a big ask- bigger than Bihar.

In Friday's no-confidence vote, the behaviour of the NDA allies that remain in the alliance- and of the BJP MPs themselves- could be guided by their own calculations for the next round of jousting, which could be round the corner if the current Monsoon session of Parliament turns out to be the last session of the present Lok Sabha.

The key question is: To what extent will they be benefited if they stand four square behind Modi? There is another question: Depending on their action on Friday, can they still bargain with BJP in the post-poll scenario if Modi does not remain its leader?

Each of these is a tricky calculation, which is anything but neat and will depend on local factors and factors that are not in the public domain, such as personal equations of members across party lines.

Given this backdrop, the natural questions that arise are: After the departure of the TDP from the fold, will NDA parties hold with the BJP? Indeed, will the BJP block itself stand without losing its composure, considering that the number of known party dissidents has grown?

At one point there were two- the famous film star-politician Shatrughan Sinha, and the well-known cricketer-politician Kirti Azad- both from Bihar. Now there are several, prominent among them being BJP's dalit MPs, including from UP, a state from which Prime Minister Narendra Modi has been elected and one that has become a major command centre of communal politics under Chif Minister Adityanath.

In addition, many BJP MPs have begun fearing the axe and may not be averse to curry favour with opposition parties in order to get their nomination to fight the next Lok Sabha election. What better opportunity than a no-confidence vote to under-write their future?

Opponents of the Narendra Modi-Amit Shah duo, including in the BJP itself, do not underestimate the strength of these very powerful and wily leaders, or their capacity to break opposition parties (the famous lure of incentives), and to bring to their side on Friday the so-called neutral elements- the AIADMK, Odisha's BJD, and Telengana's TRS.

If the voting goes meekly and along expected lines, it would mean that the BJP and the Modi camp still hasn't lost the aces in its hand. But the battle of nerves has begun.

The Wire, July 20, 2018

Resistance in the Republic of Fear

Unlike any other government that preceded it, the Narendra Modi regime has had the temerity to treat India as a plaything, and the country is resisting. This is why Modi raj is likely to go out in a dust-haze of infamy. After the Gujarat election late last year, signs of the downfall have been gathering force.

The tricks of the plutocracy now appear to work less and less. In the face of every odd, Ahmad Patel's election to the Rajya Sabha before the Gujarat Assembly polls had exposed the limits of money power summoned by the devious. This was confirmed in the recent Karnataka state election when not a single Congress or JD(S) MLA switched sides. The lotus—election symbol of Modi's party—wilted that day.

Karnataka's BJP leader had asked the governor for seven days to prove his strength in the House, but the governor gave him 15. The hand of the regime was etched large on the blatant and disgraceful plan to manipulate, or the governor—an old faithful from Gujarat—wouldn't have dared. The Supreme Court convened at 2 am to nip the mischief in the bud.

The manner in which the BJP has been run by the Narendra Modi-Amit Shah duo, the party has slowly begun to isolate itself from other political parties, including its own alliance partners. Voters too seem to be giving it the cold shoulder. The BJP's voting percentages are dropping. Soon only a tight knot of the RSS faithful is likely to remain, not much else.

We seem to be getting back to the time when the RSS-BJP used to plead with the country not to practise "political untouchability" against it. People gave them more than one chance to demonstrate that the BJP was "a party with a difference", as it loudly claimed.

Since the Atal Behari Vajpayee government had many stakeholders (it was a coalition of as many as 24 parties at one stage), the people gave Modi a clear majority of his own in Parliament so that he may give governance a good shot, but are ruing their mistake.

Now the main worry of the people seems to be how best to get the monkey off their back, and they are looking for direct and open political ways to achieve this end. They are making the democratic Opposition move in the direction of joint action against the regime.

It is a shame how things have gone on PM Modi's watch. In order to entice the people so that they may elect him as leader with adequate strength in Parliament, the RSS' chosen man promised stability and development for all. What he has delivered is the opposite.

It is no exaggeration to suggest that the present government—unlike any in the past—has unleashed anarchy. If the government had gone into the hands of the Naxalite bands, it is unlikely that greater chaos may have prevailed.

The Modi government has promoted social disorder and enmity among sections of Indians through its attitude of malign indifference when resort to violence has been taken by roaming gangs of Modi's and Shah's ideological kind in various parts of the country, especially where their party is either in power or in a situation of influence.

Indeed, on social media the PM has been reported to "follow" those with criminal intent who in the name of religion have plotted murder, and has not heeded calls to "unfollow" these unsavoury types. Armies of thousands of Hindutva thugs have been unleashed on social media in controlled fashion in order to intimidate critics of the regime, among them politicians and journalists.

The well-known television news anchor Ravish Kumar, in his newly-published book, *The Free Voice*, gives us a taste of what he has been through with thousands of so-called trolls choking his phone with threats to him and his family. The mafia tracks him. They let him know they know the routes he takes to work and tell him what they plan to do to him. They speak Hindutva language and spell out Hindutva thoughts. The police are hesitant to act.

The impression is that there can be no restraint on the thugs since they have the implied protection of those who matter. "The socialisation of fear is complete. To be afraid is to be civilised in this New Democracy," writes Kumar.

What Prime Minister in a modern democracy, which seeks to leave its impression on the world stage, will accuse his predecessor, a highly respected man, besides a former vice-president of the country and a former Army Chief, of plotting with an unfriendly neighbouring country to have him defeated in an election? Modi has done just that.

The PM disgraced his office when he said such unworthy things to the Gujarat electorate last year. This underlined his unfitness for the job. More, it subliminally appeared to sanction violence against the so-called plotters. With Modi and Shah campaigning in Gujarat with no holds barred, the BJP managed to scrape through. But what if it had lost? Would former PM Manmohan Singh and senior members of his party been made targets of hoodlum violence? This is not an idle question in the republic of fear.

Even in the recent Karnataka election, Modi said while campaigning, "Listen with your ears open, you Congressmen! I urge you to control your tongue. It is Modi you are dealing with. Watch your words or you may have to pay a heavy price."

This is a free translation in civilised English. In the original Hindi, this snatch of a speech by the PM while campaigning sounded like a dark threat of a kind heard in B-grade gangster films. The meek Dr Singh was disturbed enough to urge President Ram Nath Kovind to restrain his Prime Minister.

When such a voice is unleashed from the highest level

against the largest Opposition party in Parliament, the signal to storm-troopers is that they may do anything they like to strike fear in political opponents. But the people also hear. In the end, it is they who will return the compliments and settle the score.

In his landmark book, *Behemoth* (1942), Franz Neumann wrote that violence was "the very basis upon which the (Nazi) society rests". He called violence "the rational instrument of political power" of the fascists, and noted that it was "a technique of dominating the masses from above that served to establish totalitarian control over German society".

In just under four weeks of Hitler being appointed the German Chancellor by President Paul von Hindenburg, the fascists burnt down the German Parliament on February 27, 1933 and blamed the Communists. Within weeks, the socialists and the communists were dealt with one by one as they continued to bicker and were removed from parliament and eventually banned, hounded and killed. Fortunately, in India, the Opposition is trying to come together to challenge the strong-arm tacticians.

In an article written in 2000 for a current affairs journal, Dr Subramanian Swamy—then president of Janata Party—spoke discerningly of three prongs of a takeover bid of the RSS. The first two were demonising of those who challenge and refuse to be co-opted, and degrading the institutions of democracy so that people may lose faith in them (and become resigned to the actions of the storm-troopers later). We have witnessed the Modi government unleash the CBI, Enforcement Directorate and the taxman on the Opposition. We have also seen what's happened to the RBI, Supreme Court and Parliament (where the unheard of happened when a no-confidence motion was not permitted to be moved).

The third prong is the open subversion of the Constitution. Fortunately, we are not there yet. People power is strong enough to stop the disrupters of democracy.

Asian Age & The Deccan Chronicle, June 4, 2018

Murmurs of Discontent: Modi's Depleted Moral Capital

The time has perhaps come to inscribe *finis* under the story of the current dispensation as far as the depletion of moral capital is concerned, even if the winding up protocols must wait until Prime Minister Narendra Modi's opponents can show greater tactical awareness and the spirit of self-abnegation.

The Modi regime has lost steam because it has deviated widely from its promises. It was elected with much expectation to deepen democracy. That is what the promise of "achhe din" encapsulated in essence—the betterment of the lives of the poorest people. But in a fairly short space of time, the shape of governance began to undergo changes that bewildered its backers.

Now more and more people are beginning to worry about the overt display of authoritarian tendencies. This prime minister's mocking exercise of power has begun to cause resentment in BJP circles as well, and arrogance is being spoken of.

Naturally, Modi—lest this be overlooked—remains mindful of how he is perceived. He has not held a single press conference in four and a half years, a perverse record for a democracy. Even the outrage-causing president of the US allows himself to be questioned by a hostile media every other day. However, the PM has a one-way communication running through his "Mann Ki Baat" talks over government radio and television.

He thinks—mistakenly in light of murmurs of discontent

that can now be heard all round—that this lets him connect with his core followers direct, and that he retains his earlier popularity, affording him the room to be masterful and dismissive of senior colleagues in party and government, not just the opposition.

Of course, Modi has become increasingly conscious of late of the sheer necessity of having to show he still has a big lead over the opposition in numbers terms in parliament. Since his own party has fallen below the majority mark in the Lok Sabha after a string of recent by-election defeats in different states, the PM would be loathe to lose any more allies (after the TDP walked out of NDAand the Shiv Sena refused to vote with the government in the no-trust vote last month). There is an anxiety that if more allies renege, BJP MPs themselves may become emboldened to turn disloyal.

No government can countenance an atmosphere of such anxiety among its MPs months before the next parliament election. The sense has sharpened in the BJP camp after the recent no-confidence motion debate that the ship is going down, though the NDA won the trust vote. BJP's Dalit MPs appear especially vulnerable as the anti-Hindutva churning among Dalits outside of the BJP has emerged as a factor of note throughout the country.

The prime minister cannot afford to appear unmindful of these developments, and therefore must continue with his earlier flamboyance in attacking opponents in order to retain the affection of his allies and core constituencies. But within the BJP itself, no one now misses the obvious—that after winning a massive mandate, Modi has come to operate an oligarchy, a government by the few. All too often this boils down to a government for a few.

This means institutions do not matter and are likely to be disregarded when the need arises—in order to benefit the powerful ones or punish opponents. We saw this with the Election Commission around the time of the Gujarat assembly poll last year, and with the Supreme Court, obliging four senior judges to hold a press conference to air institutional and moral concerns.

We also see this in the clumsy political misuse by the government of the army on the issue of the so-called surgical strike which had no deterrent value. Also, newspapers are replete with stories of the CBI, Enforcement Directorate or the Income Tax machinery threatening political opponents.

In practical terms, in India, a government for a few is a plutocracy, a government of the wealthy, and a government that overlooks the interests of the poor, whatever the propaganda. The data now points in this direction.

A handful of friends of those in authority benefit from policy, but this is sought to be covered up with demagoguery, populism, ultra-nationalist slogans—on the whole, we appear to have stumbled on a regime characterised by a pursuit of selectively corporatist ideals with a few crumbs for those at the lower end. The poor are invoked out of cleverness, not with serious intent.

In Argentina, there was Eva Peron who spoke of "the shirtless"—the *descamisados*—as she pursued corporatist ends; in India there is Modi. He capitalises on the unattested story of his tea-selling origins and flies to New Delhi to take oath of office in 2014 in a private plane of an industrialist with widespread interests.

"Sab ka saath, sab ka vikas", as a slogan, was evidently a clever distraction, though initially it wasn't seen in that light. Not sending Rs 15 lakh to the bank account of every Indian has turned out to be not the only *"chunavi jumla"* (election gimmick) that BJP president Amit Shah alerted us to. The story of deepening joblessness and expanding poverty is too well-known to be re-told.

On the other hand, some perhaps can't believe their luck. In September 2016, the sudden change of the Indian partner for the Rs 59,000 crore Rafale fighter aircraft deal with France, to which Rahul Gandhi recently drew pointed attention in the Lok Sabha, tells its own story of ignominy. It may be instructive to have the issue debated threadbare in parliament followed by the appointment of a Joint Parliamentary Committee to examine the contract.

While corporate friendships now appear to go a long way, the fate of businesses as a whole does not look all that bright in the Modi raj. All other sections—the various rural classes and the urban underclass—have naturally been left to fend for themselves.

Oligarchy has taken hold in the political sphere as well. Now it is Messrs Modi and Shah all the way—a neat letterhead of political interests, which has an uncluttered past from the rough and ready Gujarat days. There was a third partner once, but he has quite literally retired hurt. It is doubtful the principals take too keen an interest in his whereabouts now, for he wasn't exactly like them.

The original duo realise elections are near, and the mood in the party is glum. The deities of the Rashtriya Swayamsevak Sangh must therefore be appeased with vigour so that the 'Hindu' battalions may be galvanised when it matters. But here too there seems a problem—an unusual one. The religious warriors may have gone soft. They have been spoilt with power, with which comes attention, and resources follow. How well does an overfed army fight?

That's the question. But the deities must continue to be propitiated. That's one reason why the mob violence that we see—the lynch mobs that mostly kill Muslims, the poor, or women in distress—cannot be stopped for now, no matter what the Supreme Court may say.

Reverence will have to be shown to cow vigilantes and those who kill and intimidate intellectual and political dissenters. They are very much a part of the political oligarchy, which is permitted to stop at nothing.

If the mob attacks began near Delhi, the heart of the sultanate, with a poor Muslim villager named Akhlaq, among the most violent recent mob attacks has been the waylaying of Swami Agnivesh, an 80-year old saffron-robed Hindu monk and social activist who has not been afraid to speak up.

The oligarchy form of political management has had a particular kind of effect in the BJP, the foremost of which is that people keep their woes to themselves and those outside the charmed circle nurse their grievance in silence. Sushma Swaraj, Nitin Gadkari, L.K. Advani sat through the recent no-trust debate impassively.

Rahul Gandhi making pointed references in the Lok Sabha to not just the Rafale contract, but also to the sudden good fortune of Shah's son, which was practically blanked out in the media, may have liberated these leading lights of the saffron (the party colour of the RSS-BJP) brigades from their fears.

The only senior to hold forth in Parliament, when the no-trust motion was debated, was Rajnath Singh, who appears to enjoy basking in reflected glory. Speaking of Rajput warriors whose lives hold a lesson, he seems to prefer the Jaichand model of acquiescence to that of Prithviraj Chauhan, who took up the challenge when he faced one.

The Wire, June 3, 2018

It's Modi vs Siddaramaiah in Karnataka

The Karnataka Assembly election at the end of this week is being widely seen as a curtain-raiser for the unfolding electoral scenario in the country, which will climax in the gladiators' contest for the next Lok Sabha. The incumbent Congress Party—the BJP's principal challenger at the national level—is no write-off in Karnataka and may therefore have expectation of better things in the future.

Such a view might not have gained ground if the BJP did not have to huff and puff in the Gujarat Assembly election only a few months ago. The two men who are seen as directly running the country under the saffron dispensation—Prime Minister Narendra Modi and BJP chief Amit Shah—conducted the election campaign in Gujarat, their home state, sidelining everyone else, including the chief minister. And yet the result, for them, was unedifying. That's when the devaluation of Modi began.

This came as a shock to the entire saffron family. The alarm bells got louder following the BJP's dreadful performance in a string of byelections in Rajasthan and Madhya Pradesh, states run by the Hindutva party. The BJP suffered humiliating defeats at the hands of the Congress, which it rightly sees as its main challenger on the national stage, rather than any of the regional parties or even a clutch of them.

The BJP's recent byelection defeats in Uttar Pradesh at the hands of the combined force of the SP and BSP served to spread panic- not just despair- in the saffron ranks. The RSS-BJP's tactics to draw in the backward castes and dalits, on whose backs were constructed the famous wins of 2014 (Lok Sabha) and early 2017 (UP Assembly), seemed to be coming apart.

Ace communalist chief minister Yogi Adityanath, who is anything but a man of God, suddenly began to be seen as a loser in Lucknow. This coincided with the waning of the Modi electoral magic after the BJP's near-defeat in Gujarat even among communally-inclined sections of the Hindu electorate.

This is the real setback for Modi and Shah. Their words carry less weight than previously. Their promises no longer ring true. Their low-grade, street-level, jibes at political opponents do not produce mirth any more.

Two separate factors have brought this about—the complete failure of the Modi government to cater to the economic well-being of Indians and the moral degradation that has set in under "India's first-ever Hindu government".

The state of the economy saps public morale on a daily basis. Farm sector woes and the plight of farmers are hitting the economy hard and throwing settled politics into turmoil. The creators of wealth and providers of employment—people who had rooted for Modi in 2014—are both chafing.

Private investment in the economy has been steadily shrinking. How can employment grow? A recent report of the well-regarded Centre for Monitoring the Indian Economy (CMIE) shows that it is not that employment hasn't expanded (that would have been a sign of an economy in good health), but that, gloomily, it has decelerated and slipped into the negative zone.

Ordinary people don't believe any more in the World Bank and the IMF data, which talk up the Indian economy. The sceptical view is that the data is sugar-coated, that the Western-controlled institutions are saying nice things about Modi's economic policies because these continue to privilege ultra-market prescriptions over public need even in a bad moment.

The sudden rise of diesel and petrol prices has begun to

colour public perceptions all the more. This comes on top of the helplessness in the system caused by bad debts of the entire banking sector, not just public sector banks. People also worry about sporadic public discussion that suggests that banks plan to charge customers from withdrawing their own money through ATMs, or for issuing cheques.

The moral degradation—now being spoken of openly in public—straddles several domains. The callousness of leading BJP figures in Jammu and UP (the Kathua and Unnao cases) have produced revulsion among ordinary folk, although the BJP remains unconcerned and resorts to sophistry.

The silence of the PM on the ghastly specifics, and his calculated failure to call a spade a spade, have perturbed even supporters. The message to the accused is that the system will help them escape the rigours of the law.

The first signs of moral questioning came with the cases of cricket entrepreneur Lalit Modi and later diamond trader Nirav Modi. Their running away from the country is now being seen as assisted departure. The names of the Rajasthan CM and the external affairs minister were openly bandied about in the Lalit Modi case. In the case of Nirav Modi, only a mildly oblique connection is being sought to be drawn with the Prime Minister via a relative and close associate of the diamond trader. The PM's refusal to speak up to defend his own honour has set tongues wagging.

Throw into the mix serious doubts raised publicly in connection with a business venture of the BJP president's son, and the evidently improper use of a top law officer of the Modi government to argue that matter in court, and a starkly disturbing picture emerges of the misuse of power for personal aggrandisement and a show of arrogant disregard for public norms and ethics.

When Karnataka voters cast their ballots on May 12, they will weigh several questions. Has the Siddaramaiah government delivered on important promises? Has it taken steps to alleviate the lot of the poor? What has it done to cope with the serious water situation affecting farmers? How deep has the corruption factor been in the government? To what extent have infrastructure needs of Bengaluru and other centres been met? And, what about the dalit question?

There will of course also be the usual political noise—and the BJP are masters of that game—about minority status for Lingayats and the dredging up of potted history around a historical figure, Tipu Sultan.

But remember, it is Modi and Shah leading the BJP's charge in Karnataka, not tainted former CM B.S. Yeddyurappa and the infamous, mines-looting Bellary brothers. The PM has, in fact, had to extend his campaigning.

Clearly, it's not the CM versus BSY; it's the CM versus PM. It's also Modi versus Congress president Rahul Gandhi, exactly as it had been in the Gujarat election, where the PM was nearly bested.

Over four years, Modi has centralised all authority that flows from political power around himself and his old-time acolyte through thick and thin, Amit Shah, as though he were a latter-day potentate. Should there be a hard landing, the familiar clapper-boys and praise-singers will melt into the shadows.

The Asian Age & The Deccan Chronicle, May 7, 2018

•

Fake News is Dirty Politics, not Journalism

Fake news" (FN), much heard of lately, is not news at all and is not part of any form of journalism. Typically, it is a part of the dirty tricks aspect of right-wing politics in many countries, as well as of intelligence outfits. The CIA has practised this dark art with consummate skill across the globe to outflank America's opponents.

Journalism casts light. It seeks to spread credible information, analysis and views without which we will flounder in today's complex and rapidly changing world. FN, on the other hand, spreads darkness. Its purpose is to confuse, spread falsehood and manipulate the unsuspecting minds of newspaper readers, television viewers and radio listeners, in order to disrupt the tempo and ethos of democratic politics.

In fact, the word "news" in its name is misleading. It should plainly be called what it is—"false information".

"False information" is related to the pursuit of retaining power or making a lunge for power in deceitful ways—by designing supposed information in a way that creates the impression of truth, and then inserting it into the mass media stream. An important aspect of FN is to show the ideological and political cohorts patronising it in favourable light.

Both aspects have been on view from the Gujarat days of Prime Minister Narendra Modi—as seen in the fixing of opponents within the BJP-RSS parivar, the clever handling of the 2002 Gujarat pogrom which is politely called the "riots", or the subject of fake encounter—and have stretching into the present.

In the Gujarat Assembly poll campaign last year, the PM himself practised FN when he publicly accused his predecessor Manmohan Singh, former vice-president Hamid Ansari, and a retired Army Chief, of conspiring with Pakistan to have him defeated. The Donald Trump election campaign for the US presidency practised FN successfully with the aid of a network of far-right and white supremacist interest groups and websites.

Since Hitler, fake news has been shown to be the mainstay of rightist plots to deflect criticism and to discredit and confuse opponents. The genius of Goebbels, the Fuehrer's minister for propaganda and a vile man, is well known. The recipe he advanced was simply to cook up "facts" and then getting these repeated a hundred times so that people may believe them.

Once that comes to pass, to correct the situation and bring about disbelief in the false information—by now flowing freely in the mass media—becomes an uphill task. In our present day, such dangerous false stuff circulates wildly through the social media, such as WhatsApp, and is virtually impossible to roll back.

It is a pity our television stations do what they can to put a cloak over reality. Typically they catch someone from the Congress (or any Opposition party) and a person each from the RSS as well as the BJP (misleading us into believing they are different things) to be on the same debate panel on FN, but discuss good journalism versus dishonest journalism—failing to point out that fake news is not dishonest journalism but no journalism. It is an altogether different species.

Smriti Irani, the information and broadcasting minister, has expressed her desire to fight fake news. All power to her elbow. But the way she is speaking, it appears she'd go after news and views on the Web, 80 per cent of which is created by established media houses (who follow the rules and procedures of good journalism) or by thorough professionals.

She doesn't speak of cleaning up the cesspool of the social

media. But she could make a refreshing new start by telling us about Shilpi Tewari in the context of the scandal about doctored videos to bring into disrepute JNU student leaders in February-March of 2016, when Irani was I&B minister.

According to a report in an English daily in March 2016 (such news items also appeared elsewhere), Tewari's Twitter account hosted some of these videos which were uploaded on YouTube. These purported to show that then JNU president Kanhaiya Kumar was "caught shouting anti-national slogans".

A forensic report commissioned by the Delhi government showed that the videos were manipulated to create a certain effect. Tewari dropped out of sight. The English daily quoted an I&B ministry spokesman to say that Tewari may be "assisting" Irani on a "private basis", and that she had been offered an official position but had not taken it.

A volume was published last year, which detailed how the BJP produced propaganda on an industrial scale against political opponents and ideological antagonists. Its most prominent target was Rahul Gandhi. The book, written by a participant in the exercise whose conscience began to prick and she defected, speaks of the massive effort that went into making the whole country believe for a long time that Gandhi was a "pappu"—a duffer.

This was sophisticated FN meant to degrade a key opponent before battle is joined, in the spirit of the teachings of Sun Tzu, the Chinese strategist who taught that the enemy should be defeated before it takes the field. The book was practically ignored in the Indian media—no doubt out of fear of the ruling establishment—but was reported at length in the Guardian, a famous British newspaper.

Modi romped home victorious in May 2014. But his campaign for Delhi had begun well before that—with FN. In August 2011 then Congress chief Sonia Gandhi went to the US for a surgery. She was again in America in the first week of September 2012 for treatment. Shortly afterward, the future Prime Minister was already attacking the Congress Party and asking questions of then PM Manmohan Singh. He claimed (without credible basis) that the Government of India had spent rupees 1,880 crores of public money on Sonia Gandhi's medical treatment, Firstpost.com reported on October 3, 2012.

The basis of the astounding claim was apparently a newspaper report which had relied on a RTI application. It was plain to see that a convenient news item had been "planted" in a shoddy publication so that the BJP leader may later be enabled to allude to it in order to paint his chief opponent as corrupt.

The air was cleared when then chief information commissioner Satyanand Mishra officially replied to a RTI query by one Naveen Kumar from Moradabad that the GoI had not paid for the Congress president's treatment abroad. In four years as PM, Modi has been unable to substantiate his sensational claim.

In 2012, the present PM sought to use FN to tarnish his Congress adversary. After he became the PM, his party mounted an extensive FN campaign to portray Mr Gandhi as foolish and unfit for politics, and now FN sites are being used to discredit top quality news that's critical of the Modi government.

At least one of these, The True Picture, has reportedly been endorsed by 13 of Mr Modi's ministers. This is a clear sign of desperation at a time when five dalit BJP MPs from Uttar Pradesh have written to the PM complaining of the BJP's attitude towards dalits. The political space is opening up.

Asian Age & The Deccan Chronicle, April 9, 2018

No Confidence to Even Stand in Front of a Mirror

Since the Modi dispensation is not above disregarding convention and rules (it smuggled in its fundamentally altered Aadhaar template as a money bill in order to escape scrutiny in the Rajya Sabha where its numbers were deficient), it should occasion little surprise if Lok Sabha speaker Sumitra Mahajan does not allow the no-confidence motion for which notices have been given.

Ordinarily, if procedurally sound in terms of having the backing of at least 50 MPs, a no-confidence motion must be taken up at the first opportunity—in this case on Monday morning, as the Lok Sabha meets.

But the opposition, which is on the warpath, can't bet on this. A simple trick is all that is needed to be performed. Since there aren't so many working days left before the budget session ends, with the help of some of its supporters the BJP can finesse the movers of the motion with ease by citing unruliness in the house.

If the house is not brought to order, a no-confidence motion cannot be taken up. And of course the Speaker—the good sport—may be expected to shrug her helplessness. In the record books, the episode will take its place among a long list of unprecedented happenings in the time of Prime Minister Narendra Modi.

The BJP's majority in the Lok Sabha is far from eroded, but the government is breaking into a sweat. It is doubtless aware that its stock in the country has sunk after the near defeat in Gujarat, the private turf of *pradhan sevak* (literally, prime servant of the people) Modi and his *pratham sevak* (literally, the firse servant), Amit Shah. The electoral ambush by the rural folk of Gujarat was followed in quick succession by humiliations in parliamentary and assembly by-elections across the Hindi heartland of Rajasthan, Madhya Pradesh and now Bihar and Uttar Pradesh. These are electoral geographies which had made Modi prime minister and where the RSS is said to have magical powers.

It is the clear lack of ambiguity in the situation that is so compelling. There is little doubt that the government has the numbers. The no-confidence motion will be roundly defeated in case it is permitted to be moved. And yet the regime is running for cover.

The reason is that lack of confidence in the Modi power vertical has been expressed in black and white by a party—the TDP—which only a week earlier was part of the ruling dispensation and had been buddies with the BJP for close on two decades.

In fewer than four lurching years of Modi rule, this spells a crisis of credibility for the saffron brigade whose reverberations will be felt at least until the next Lok Sabha election. And even afterwards, it may become commonplace to hear how the BJP has a policy of use-and-throw for allies. This makes the RSS-BJP untrustworthy partners. That's a dreadful reputation to have.

The TDP moving the no-trust motion lays bare the fragilities that abound within the BJP-led NDA. This is why permitting the motion to be debated on the floor of parliament is likely to be more than a mere embarrassment as colour will start running from carefully dry-cleaned drapes, and the nation will watch the spectacle live on television.

This could also be a moment for the Shiv Sena, another coalition partner of the BJP, to perk up and give its dagger another turn. The SS, which is the BJP's government partner in Maharashtra but is always looking for ways to string up its cocky ally, has still not opened its hand.

For the BJP, the dread remains that the Sena could vote with TDP and against the government. Even if that doesn't come to pass, the Sena's representative could spit venom when he rises to speak on the no-trust motion and the BJP will have no place to hide.

To end any of these possibilities from taking shape, all that the government need do is to use tricks to bypass the no-confidence motion and bring the budget session to a close after rushing through the formalities of passing the appropriations Bill amidst noise and walk-outs since the Lok Sabha has already cleared the finance Bill—without debate, taking advantage of sustained disturbances in both Houses.

It is worth pondering if any of this really matters in the end. The government's name is mud already. The youth can't find work. Industry is facing serious problems. Agriculture is in crisis. Farmers have agitated in different places and have been shot at by the police. Not many days ago, about 50,000 dead poor tribal farmers from the interiors of Maharashtra marched for a week to pour into Mumbai with cracked and swollen feet to press their demands.

They waved the red banner of the communists but residents of Maximum City—home to India's industry and finance—gave them an affectionate welcome. Even the Shiv Sena, ideological creatures of a regional variety of Hindutva, met the marchers with sympathy. The rural-urban gap was bridged. The message is: the people are rising. Tricks played in parliament may become just a footnote for the clerks to record.

When the heartland has been blasted open, who remembers Tripura, except for the felling of the Lenin statue, and the meaningful silence of the prime minister which was broken only when a bust of Syama Prasad Mukherjee, the founder of the Jana Sangh- BJP's precursor- was laid low in Kolkata by vandals in another despicable act?

Lenin was a friend of the Indian people when they were up

against colonial rule. He had advised the Indian communists—debunking M.N. Roy's thesis—to pipe down and get in step with Gandhi's mass movement. But the Sangh *parivar* only remembered him as a "foreigner" and proclaimed that their India can have no place for such a man.

However, there is, in their scheme of things, no place for Gandhi either. Nirmal Kumar Bose, the great anthropologist and culturist and Gandhi's secretary when the Mahatma visited Noakhali to quell communal blood-letting with his moral force, had this to say about Gandhi and Lenin: "In the midst of gloom which encircles mankind on all sides, there are always men who struggle with the surrounding darkness.... Of such men in the present age, we can think of two who successfully fought the battle...Lenin and Gandhi."

In parliament, Modi has a strong suit. That's a story worth tracking. But outside, the people are on the move.

The Wire, March 19, 2018

Why an Early Election Has Become a Political Compulsion for Narendra Modi

Rulers seldom know what's happening, do they? They have the intelligence apparatus and their party politicos feeding them whatever the powerful like to hear, but the assessment of the people can be in delicious discord.

Atal Bihari Vajpayee ordered elections early because his India was shining. He paid the price. Through cries of policy paralysis and corruption, Manmohan Singh went in expecting to be reasonably rewarded. After all, his government had delivered a nearly 7-8% (9-10% by today's yardstick) rate of growth over most of his ten-year period, unprecedented for a democracy. Yet, the result was a shock.

What was common between the two governments—covering a period of about 16 years of elite section boy-scout optimism—was bubbly talk for much of the time by economists, policy wonks, and the World Bank and the IMF. In the end, the politics probably turned on a less talked about variable: jobless growth, which analysts hadn't troubled themselves with.

In the strapped situation of lukewarm private sector investment we are in today, and the major employment-generating informal economy sector having taken a hit since demonetisation, no analyst or political planner can afford to overlook jobless growth.

Pakora growth (the espousal of energetic vending of a popular snack as a substitute for job creation, a notion that was rightly ridiculed)- a close enough synonym- staring the country in the face is hardly a pleasing outcome after four years of "game-changing" economics, no matter how combatively BJP chief Amit Shah defended it in his maiden speech in the Rajya Sabha.

Young Indians of any class, on whose shoulders rides the much-vaunted promise of the demographic dividend, are not amused. Rampant joblessness is a feature the Modi sarkar shares with the governments of Vajpayee and Singh. Alas, what it does not share with their time in office is a long patch of striking expansion of the economy.

Not to put too fine a point on it, we now find ourselves stuck in a time of creeping pessimism, although international capital has done its best to talk up the India story through friendly statements issued by the IMF and the World Bank that the Modi regime perversely quotes all the time, though it only has to look around to find the truth.

What's worse, India is slipping when the US and Europe have recovered and when the international price of oil is still in benign territory.

The dim economic outlook is likely to impose a cut-and-run political strategy on the prime minister, although MPs in general, not just of the ruling party, do not like their term cut short.

For Modi, an early election is, therefore, likely to be a political compulsion. In this respect, his story is different from that of Vajpayee's. The latter had chosen to go to the country early of his own volition in order to seize what his advisors thought might be a bright moment.

The contrast in circumstances Modi finds himself in has been accentuated by the morale-sapping defeat in the recent by-elections in Rajasthan. Ordinarily, losing by-elections is not the end of the world, although ruling parties frequently coast to easy victories in them. However, the BJP lost every one of the 16 Assembly segments that make up the Lok Sabha constituencies of Alwar and Ajmer.

That is a lot of territory to lose in one go and should be

a distinct worry for the saffron party. Rajasthan has an old and active RSS network, which in recent times was lubricated through political and social actions of the Hindutva variety, most notably cow vigilante actions. But none of this counted with the voter.

The "secular" realm—jobs, prices, the economy, living conditions—trumped the world of perverse ideas delivered slickly through clever propaganda disseminated not just by fanatical Hindutva outfits but also a section of the fawning media.

Assembly elections in Rajasthan, Madhya Pradesh and Chhatisgarh are due in December this year and the Lok Sabha poll should in the normal course be held in April-May, 2019. However, when the prognosis for the BJP in these states is none too bright (remember the bad news began to pour in from Modi's home state Gujarat, where BJP's win was so tenuous that the party cannot even celebrate it), and the Rajasthan byelection rresults hammered home a bitter truth, can the prime minister risk holding the Lok Sabha election after a potentially weak showing in three BJP-ruled states?

This will be the singular consideration guiding the prime minister if he decides to go to the country early, not some high-intentioned thinking on the presumed benefits to the country of holding parliament and state polls simultaneously.

The year 2017 began brilliantly for Modi and Amit Shah with a staggering win in Uttar Pradesh. But the year ended on a sobering note on account of the factors that became evident first in Gujarat and then in Rajasthan—rampant joblessness, farmers' plight, the woes of the working classes in the 'rurban' areas and in cities proper. If a week is a long time in politics, a year is an eternity.

The Wire, Feburay 18, 2018

A Heartless Idea of India

"New India" is Prime Minister Narendra Modi's copyright. It wasn't in the BJP manifesto in 2014. It is a powerful rubric with which to attract youth power, and harness it.

And yet, when nearly four years of the five are done, the best that Mr Modi's BJP can do to bring the young Indian on board is to cook up the idiotic notion of "pakora" growth, and pakora politics, when unemployment is rampant among all classes.

This little savoury on the snack menu can't surely be the lead symbol of the Asian century in which India thinks it has a part to play. Vending pakoras can hardly be said to the real meaning of India in the new era.

But, surprisingly, Modi believes it does. When questions on rising joblessness were being flung at him, he was far from defensive. His instinctive—and instant and heartless—reply was that making pakoras was also work.

It is hard not to be reminded of the vicious mocking tone of Marie Antoinette—the French queen sent to the guillotine by the revolutionaries, and known for her taste for fancy clothes—when she said if Frenchmen could not eat bread, let them eat cakes.

The Modi government's achievement on the front of meaningful employment for the young people is less than shallow. The PM in all honesty can't point to employment or self-employment gains flowing from the much-hyped official programmes such as Skill India, Stand Up India, or the BHIM app spinning out processes that lead to gainful work for the youth in keeping with the aspirations of our times, which Mr Modi's rhetorical highs helped fuel.

The employment data is woeful. This should cause no surprise, windbag speeches aside. When private investment figures for the economy signal long-time lows, even a "service-sector" avenue like selling hot pakoras cannot have seen a massive expansion. Besides, there is not much value-addition involved in such a line of work, and the earnings are pitiable—hardly an advertisement for the shining glory promised in craftily designed government ads and slogans.

BJP president Amit Shah is the perfect acolyte and follows very closely in his master's footstep. Thus, hardly had Modi uttered pakora than Shah take up the idea with a devotee's passion. He held forth on pakora employment in his maiden Rajya Sabha speech last week, attacking political opponents for mocking this as an example of meaningful economic activity.

Let not a national party—the country's ruling party—degrade itself in this manner because it has failed to live up to its promise of building the economy and seeking to expand it in directions that will yield a new future for young Indians.

It's a disgrace and leaves a terrible impression of the country—not just of the BJP—among people around the world at a time when the BJP is planning to designate Modi a "Global Legend", no less.

For doing what exactly? Who knows? May be for getting the saffron party to have a parliamentary majority of its own, for there is no evidence whatsoever of this Indian Prime Minister leaving the slightest mark on the world stage—with his neighbourhood policy a shambles, and the relationship with America dependent only on selling India as a huge market and a military base.

But for a party always on the lookout for propaganda punches, the PM is the new Nehru, the new Gandhi, the new Mao, the new Dalai Lama and even the new Marilyn Monroe rolled in one. However, propaganda fades and falsehood has a narrow shelf life; reality lives on.

Last heard, the BJP was planning pakora parties and opening pakora stalls in a miserable attempt to mock the Opposition and to subliminally suggest to the poor that the saffron party's opponents were making fun of them for doing low-value work. This is "technology for development" of the Modi era.

"Chaiwala" politics is long done. If the Prime Minister must offer the country hope, he must move on and invent fresh gags and new lines of enchantment. Modi has gone places on the strength of volatile, hypocritical, speeches delivered mostly in the idiom of the poor Indian. These were aimed at self-glorification and the denigration of others in unbecoming language. People have seen through them, especially the poor who had swallowed the untruths and were fooled. It's time to move on.

Mostly these speeches were constructed on the basis of "facts"—either so-called current data or presumed historical information—that were manufactured to dupe the unsuspecting public in an era when many Indians derive their information almost solely from WhatsApp groups, treating the abounding rumours contained in them as gospel.

Even by his own troubling standards, the PM's reply in parliament to the motion of thanks to the President's address last week was startling. It made evident that Modi's principal agenda is to pull down Nehru and banish him even from the land of memory; it is not to create jobs or promote science and learning or better lives for Indians.

The agenda is to build a "New India" of the RSS' imagination. Plainly put, the idea is to assert that all the science we know is embedded in the Vedas, and to deny that non-Hindu Indians had any contribution in the making of India's culture and civilisation.

In this "New India", Deendayal Upadhyay, a deep votary of RSS' fundamental tenets, which demonise Gandhi and his work, is the new Gandhi. Nehru's vision stands in the way of this egregious project. Hence, it must be denigrated even by inventing history, as Modi did in Parliament.

To challenge the reasonable notion that it is hard to think of democracy without Nehru, the PM expounded that India had democracy even in the Lichchavi era!

Then, the usual Patel card: If Vallabhbhai were PM, there will be no Kashmir problem. No one has informed Modi that both Nehru and Patel had together told Maharaja Hari Singh that it won't be considered an anti-India act even if he chose to join Pakistan, but he should make up his mind before Independence came about.

And no one's informed Modi that it is Gandhi who made Nehru PM and that he didn't usurp the throne. Anyway, it is now too late for Narendrabhai to change. May be the people will change him.

Asian Age & The Deccan Chronicle, February 12, 2018

Nation on the Mat as Modi Wins

For Prime Minister Narendra Modi and the BJP ruling setup in the country, which he personally exemplifies, the current year has been ushered in on a belittling note. As the previous year was turning, Modi won a victory in Gujarat which his party just cannot celebrate, given its mocking nature. And, just when the year turned, official data suggested that under this leader the country has registered its lowest economic growth in four years.

It is becoming increasingly clear that practically everything that Modi touched has turned to mud. The former RSS *pracharak*, or full-time volunteer, was evidently born with a good luck charm. The first time he entered the Gujarat assembly was as chief minister, and the first time he entered parliament was as Prime Minister, as he has himself proudly informed us.

But this personal luck has not translated to luck for the country, as mindless initiatives have turned sour, demonetisation being a perfect example. Modi will be remembered as a PM in whose tenure economic miseries were piled on the people even as the glue of social and cultural cohesion that joined different sections of society was forced unstuck through violence by lumpen squads unrestrained by the hand of the law.

Not all the prayers to Lord Vishwanath in Kashi, Mr Modi's parliamentary constituency, are likely to help him. Bhole Baba cannot be pleased with the unholy goings-on in Modi's India. The Lord has a mind of his own. It cannot be bent by threats or blandishments from keepers of the Gorakhnath Mutt in UP or from Amit Shah, who is the real Master-of-Rolls—no matter what the Chief Justice of India may think—when it comes to keeping the judiciary on a tight leash—in Gujarat or elsewhere.

Modi in 2014 had the *brahmastra*—the ultimate weapon of Hindu mythology—in his hand, bestowed by a once-in-a-generation parliamentary majority. With it he could defeat any enemy of the people he chose to.

Instead, he focused on little things, and on shadows that did not exist but were cooked up and labelled as enemies by the RSS. The real enemies—unemployment, poverty, farmers' distress, the woes of the small entrepreneur—weren't even touched.

This is because the PM proved incapable of 21st century imagination. He couldn't think big. His poverty of ideas restricted him to small talk in a big voice on radio broadcasts on Sundays, and he vowed to destroy his opponents. This was on full display when he accused the Congress Party of conspiring with Pakistan to win the Gujarat election. He focused more on the silliest things like building the tallest statue of Sardar Vallabhbhai Patel. Even this didn't cut ice with the voters of Gujarat.

The Narendra Modi raj has alienated the country. This wasn't immediately evident as he acted under the cover of religious symbolisms of Hinduism, the faith of the majority in the country, with which simple people were taken in. But it is in the nature of rot to spread.

This present Prime Minister inherited an economy that, on average, had grown just under eight per cent a year for 10 years even with a conspicuous slowdown toward the end.

The global outlook too was propitious with oil prices at a record low, a luxury his predecessor didn't have. This is the political equivalent of being born with a silver spoon in the mouth. But Modi blew it.

Businesses have not grown since May 2014 when the Modi

government took office. Industrial performance has dipped. Green shoots of recovery that occasionally show up—as is the case right now—wilt before the day turns to night.

The urban middle classes, the BJP's principal supporters, will be thrown sops in the forthcoming Budget because a clutch of state elections are around the corner and the BJP-led government must prepare for the Lok Sabha polls in early 2019, but will these help retain their affection as the economy slips and joblessness and prices take their toll?

How far can the stunt of invoking Hindu mythology and the promise of Hindu power—as a conscious counterpoise to the poison of Islamist beliefs—really go?

The trick of getting by with calling opponents corrupt has also lost its sting after the so-called 2G scam devised by an evidently motivated Comptroller and Auditor-General of India was roundly decried in a recent court order. The CBI is so discredited that it can't summon the nerve to challenge this verdict.

Rural society is in the middle of being turned upside down. After a lag of some years, we had a good monsoon in 2016. But the harebrained scheme of demonetisation wiped out any chance there may have been of seizing the momentum.

Agriculture and the informal sector, which provide the bulk of jobs and export earnings, are struggling with negative expectations, especially after the ill-considered implementation of a poorly-crafted Goods and Services Tax, touted as the next best thing after India's independence, and inaugurated as such with high ceremony at the midnight hour in the Central Hall of Parliament last July in an un-historical, unbecoming and grotesque mimicking of the midnight glory over 70 years ago when Jawaharlal Nehru rose to speak in high cadence of India coming to "life and freedom", as the Union Jack was lowered for the last time in India and the tricolour unfurled.

Modi has won. But the country is on the mat. The promise of *achche din*—or better times—now strikes people as a compact that was not meant to be honoured. It rings hollow today.

To recall Shah's incomparably cunning words, it was no more than a part of a throwaway, election-time jumla (sentence).

We are in a social mess, and the economic front remains dispiriting. But matters are a lot worse. Brazenly discriminatory actions are being taken against the poor. Indian workers headed to the Gulf for their livelihood will have a different colour of passport from the rest of us. Institutions are being subverted.

The Supreme Court is in the news. Just before the Gujarat poll, the Election Commission was up to lousy tricks which fooled no one. Democracy in India is being pushed to the wall.

Asian Age & The Deccan Chronicle, January 16, 2018

2G Verdict: The Ghost of Five Christmases Past

Politics does not run in linear ways. And the 2G spectrum verdict delivered by a special CBI court on Thursday kind of substantiates this.

When the stock of the BJP—and that of Prime Minister Narendra Modi—appears to have suffered a dip in the backdrop of the recent Gujarat assembly poll, the Congress would naturally argue that the story of the '2G spectrum allocation scandal' was a massive propaganda frame-up against the Manmohan Singh-led UPA government.

After all, it was this that had set the stage for a massive BJP campaign against the Congress in the run-up to the 2014 parliamentary polls. Its leitmotif was that the Congress, as a party, engenders corruption. It was a whirling campaign on these lines- ignoring the fact that the Manmohan Singh government had delivered economic growth of more than 7% over a 10-year period, a record for a democracy—which went a long way in handing the Congress its worst drubbing in 70 years in 2014.

Will the main Opposition party be believed in the public realm after the judgement of the special court? That depends. If the disenchantment at the level of ordinary people—triggered by GoI's policies or their implementation—continues to grow at the present rate, it is the BJP that is not likely to be believed when it resuscitates its battle-cry of Congress being the 'kingpin' of corruption.

And matters can get a lot worse if over the coming

months, the BJP doesn't perform to its potential in the states it rules—Rajasthan, Madhya Pradesh and Chhattisgarh—and if it cannot wrest back Karnataka from the Congress. This is a state in which BJP has had a strong presence in the recent past.

It was a Supreme Court-directed probe that culminated in Thursday's verdict which showed that GoI agencies just did not manage to prove the charge of criminality made against A. Raja, the telecom minister from the DMK quota under the UPA regime, and DMK MP MK Kanimozhi, daughter of DMK patriarch M Karunanidhi, besides 17 others, including top civil servants and representatives of business groups.

To keep its own credibility alive, GoI has little choice but to move an appeal in the High Court against the judgment of the special CBI court. However, this does carry risks. If the apex court has monitored the probe, then it would appear that the CBI and the Enforcement Directorate have already put their best foot forward, and may not have too much more to offer at the appeal stage.

A setback at the appellate level is likely to create a Hamletian dilemma for the government. 'To do or not to do?' is the question. The relief that the special court's order has given to senior functionaries of the DMK has the potential to turn Tamil Nadu politics topsyturvy, especially given the straits both the AIADMK as a party and the AIADMK government find themselves in.

Many will doubtless watch if the BJP continues to try to cosy up to the DMK to be on the probable winning side in the state after the death of J Jayalalithaa (whom the BJP had wooed assiduously despite corruption charges against her), its efforts stymied only by her death. That may tell on the BJP's credibility.

The report of the Comptroller and Auditor General (CAG), a constitutional body, on the alleged 2G scam had lent a ring of truth to the allegation. In its wake, the Anna Hazare campaign and other protestss had hit the Manmohan Singh regime where it hurt most. When the UPA 2 government went into a tailspin, 'policy paralysis' followed. The skies crashed around the UPA regime.

The special CBI court judgement invites us to interrogate the principal political passages of the past five years.

Economic Times, December 22, 2017

Business as Usual Not Possible for BJP

The BJP has been stunned by the Gujarat results but is doing what it can to put up a brave face. The Congress has lost, but the defeat has a bitter-sweet quality about it.

There were times in the see-saw battle, as the votes were being counted, when a slim Congress victory did not appear far-fetched. The last dozen or so seats for which votes were tallied could have gone either way, so tight were the margins.

The changed tone of an otherwise fiercely partisan and perennially "pro-national" television anchors, who bow and scrape before the pettiest in the saffron brigade, left nothing to the imagination. The loud-mouthed and ultra-aggressive BJP leaders, whose braggadocio had scaled embarrassing heights after the exit polls, suddenly appeared subdued.

There is prospect in the circumstances thrown up by Gujarat of a return to capture lost ground by anti-Hindutva forces in states including the BJP-ruled states of Rajasthan, Madhya Pradesh and Chhattisgarh where Assembly polls are due in a few months. These set up the scaffolding for Lok Sabha 2019.

The most important outcome of the election in Gujarat is that it has raised the sights of a new turn in politics in the country which only weeks earlier had appeared improbable. The new Congress president Rahul Gandhi deserves every bit of credit for bringing about this transitional stage.

Gandhi skillfully guided the atmosphere of political insurrection in Gujarat brought about by the unremitting energies of Hardik Patel who was not old enough even to contest the election, and Alpesh Thakore and Jignesh Mevani. All three are household names now.

They are not cut from the same cloth but their political design was clear. It was to defeat the BJP because the so-called Gujarat model of development stinks. Hardik, Alpesh and Jignesh became a living proof that the economic model of Prime Minister Narendra Modi works against the poor and that it is for the very rich, and that's the reason it is being pushed with uncommon zeal.

This was the reality on the ground based on which the revolt of ordinary Gujaratis was constructed, giving the BJP a torrid time. The RSS-BJP knows the story of Haldighati well. The heroic Bhil archers of Gujarat were Hardik, Alpesh and Jignesh. Without them the stage would not have been set, just as without Pratap there would be no action on the stage. It is not a case of one or the other.

Leaders sometimes create the circumstances of their glory. Sometimes, they enter upon a specific situation and transform the scene. The incendiary circumstances present in Gujarat are the products of Modi's actions. In this state specially, several examples can be found of the pampering of big industry, and the short-changing of ordinary people and of the lower tiers of trade, business and industry, and of farmers and workers.

Jobs are hard to come by. Conditions have been created for the alienation of farmers' lands to be transferred to industry and the former tillers of land swell the ranks of the unemployed.

Evidently, this time round in Gujarat the scurrilous hate propaganda relying on dog-whistle tactics—one day featuring a young woman arriving home safely but breathless as the Muslim call for prayer is sounded; another day, the accusing of a Sikh former Prime Minister, a Muslim former vice-president and a Hindu former Army chief, of colluding with Pakistan to defeat Modi in Gujarat—cut no ice. This makes it clear that for the proponents of Hindutva politics, it cannot be business as usual any more.

The challenge has arrived. It concerns the burdens of everyday living—prices, unemployment, the miseries faced by farmers and workers and the policy imperatives needed to deliver affordable healthcare, education and homes. These are "secular" issues, or matters of everyday concern, not linked to religion.

For these, Hindutva—the vehicle of political Hinduism—has no answers. The saffron brigade simply does not understand the expression "secular". It foolishly mocks it. Its skill-set and class-orientation do not equip it to deal with the complexities involved in solving questions of liberal and "secular" politics and economics that aims to cut and end mass poverty.

In lieu of grappling with such complexities, Hindutva uses the alchemy of befuddling the people with cultural nationalism, pride in the military way of life and unfurling of the national flag at the drop of a hat. But these failed to impress in Gujarat in the way they used to. Something has changed and this will be BJP's worry now.

The voter in Gujarat has just telegraphed Modi and his acolyte Amit Shah to say that he does not need their certificate of patriotism and that he mastered the configuration behind the sentiment of "Bharat Mata" long before Hindutva arrived on the scene. If the challenge to the BJP has arrived in the shape of the demands of secular life, the challenger too has arrived in the shape of Gandhi.

What the new Congress president makes of the opportunity is to be seen, however. Does he have the largeness of imagination to take along all who wish to come along, and not be side-tracked by small-time bickering of everyday politics?

Asian Age & The Deccan Chronicle, December 20, 2017

Gujarat Polls: It's All About Modi, No One Else

The Gujarat model of development was the flavour of the poll season in 2014 when then chief minister Narendra Modi rode to power in New Delhi. It was with a magician's enthusiasm for the tricks up his sleeve that Modi had rolled out the "Gujarat model" in election meetings around the country, even if it wasn't explained what it meant.

But in the current campaign for the assembly polls in Gujarat, this "model" appears to be a noteworthy absence, though it was once presumed to be synonymous with "spectacular", and had apparently brought the people of Gujarat untold happiness.

The BJP dare not wheel it out in this election season, fearing undesirable repercussions. Everyone has now understood that no such "model" existed at all, and that Modi had only produced a conjurer's trick. So widely ridiculed is the idea today that even the Opposition Congress doesn't think it worthwhile to make pointed negative references to it.

The Ro-Ro ferry service that the PM inaugurated in his home state in the midst of the current poll campaign was a reminder, if one was needed, of the extraordinary slowness of Modi's development efforts in his home state—the so-called "Gujarat model"—which in some sectors appears to be even more anaemic than the Bihar model that usually brings forth a good-natured laugh. The service had been conceived years ago when Modi was CM and was late by a decade coming.

The plight of the traditionally landowning and prosperous

Patels or Patidars, now fighting for quotas in education and jobs, is yet another reminder that the "Gujarat model" had no basis in fact and was no more than a craftily contrived hoax to dupe voters in Modi's bid for power in Delhi.

How the Gujarat electorate outside of the nicely comfortable urban middleclass milieu responds in this election to the dubious claims of development in two decades of BJP rule, much of the time under Modi, the BJP's high-pitched salesman, will be interesting to watch. It is the Modi charisma that's on trial—no two ways about it.

It is noteworthy that BJP top gun Amit Shah appears a sobered man these days and has lately refrained from repeating the slogan of "150 plus" for his party in an assembly of 182. He has clearly absorbed the lessons of his disastrous attempts at holding campaign meetings a few weeks ago when he was heckled by fellow Gujaratis. The extreme curiosity that his son's business dealings have aroused shrinks his elbow-room further.

In contrast, PM Modi, who is giving the campaign everything he has got, still draws crowds. He is, in fact, said to be the lynchpin of the BJP in the state, not just the face of its election effort. Local observers report inner turmoil in the Gujarat BJP. This is among the reasons why the PM is lining up cabinet ministers, including a former television actress, to dazzle the voter with.

Nevertheless, the question asked is: 'Take Modi out of the equation, and where is the BJP?" The much-vaunted RSS organisation is not to be scoffed at, and yet uncertainty gnaws at the saffron party, although the campaign on the other side is being run by Rahul Gandhi, who was being treated as a walkover till the other day. Evidently, it is not just a reinvigorated Gandhi that the ruling party is up against, but an electorate that the Congress leader finds responsive and Shah doesn't.

It is hard to tell where all this will lead. But one thing is evident. The ruling BJP's campaign is not about the so-called achievements of its 22-year-old rule in Gujarat, or even the failures of the Congress elsewhere—except in sweeping terms, such as attacks on Jawaharlal Nehru and the hardy perennial "dynasty" barb.

The saffron party's campaign is about Gandhi the individual, with a denigration of him as being insufficiently knowledgeable about Hindu religious customs and traditions. This is the ultra-nationalistic discourse all over again, behind which lurks communal politics.

Since the chief Congress campaigner cannot any more be made fun of as one lacking in grey matter, the question that top BJP leaders—including Union cabinet ministers and the saffron-robed UP chief minister Yogi Adityanath—like to ask these days is why the Congress vice-president is visiting temples, and whether he even knows how to pray, Hindu-style, which is a roundabout way of pressing the familiar Hindu nationalism agenda.

Since the RSS-BJP came to power at the Centre three years ago riding the buggy of Hindu communalism, and using religious imagery to propel itself and denounce its opponents as being not just anti-Hindu but also anti-religion, anti-national and anti-India, the Congress' Gujarat campaign seems to have readjusted its tactics so as not to permit the BJP a monopoly over "Hindu tradition", and thus give it yet another chance to tar opponents as being "anti-religion" and take the discussion away from everyday existence concerns, especially of the unprivileged, on which the BJP's record in government is substandard.

Therefore, Gandhi's temple visits in Gujarat are causing the saffron leadership considerable unease. The BJP-RSS have no answer to his query: "Can't I visit a temple?"

The ruling party is finding its trump card is being degraded, and has floated a clever sub-rosa campaign—that Gandhi is running on a "soft-communal" platform. Hard secularists used to say these sorts of things once, but now the BJP is getting into the act.

There is some historical irony here. Not all those who go to a temple or a mosque are communal. Indians understand this better than most as most Indians are religious but not communal. Therefore, a visit to a religious place by a political leader tends to be measured in the right register by voters, but mischievously by its opponents.

The logic and rule of politics is clear: A show of religious symbolism slips into communal conduct only when it is a part of a strategy of mobilising a particular religious community for political or ideological ends and, typically, in opposition to other religious denominations; not otherwise. But even if temples are being visited, it's not the Lord of Dwarkapeeth who will decide the election, it is the ordinary voter.

Asian Age & The Deccan Chronicle, November 20, 2017

Sheen off Modi Raj, Rahul's Path Rocky

Rahul Gandhi- derided as soft in the head by a committed but unprincipled social media army (directed by an invisible hand), with sniper support from regulars- stunned detractors when he made quite a decent speech at the University of California in Berkeley recently.

He answered probing questions from the campus audience with candour, unlike devious politicians who are deemed serious and capable as they offer opaque answers with double meanings that send out self-congratulatory messages to followers and mean threats to opponents. Throughout, the Congress leader displayed a lack of rancour, a touch of wit, and due regard for decorum.

This was enough to set the cat among the pigeons. Heavy artillery was deployed to dismantle Gandhi, although the Congressman is routinely lampooned as inadequate and inept by the BJP-RSS. BJP chief Amit Shah made a quick jab below the belt. A cabinet minister aimed poison darts. Smriti Irani, a regime favourite, used her cabinet position to hog television time as she shot missiles dripping with venom at the Congress leader.

This comes naturally to Irani, who made bold to assert that while some people had to work hard to reach where they'd got, the dynast had got everything on a platter. Naturally, people are curious to know in what positions this minister has toiled to bag plum cabinet posts after losing her Lok Sabha election.

It is clear to everyone—even Narendra Modi's cabinet

colleagues—that the PM couldn't have pulled off the trick that RG did at Berkeley. He is short on intellectual fibre. He is good at something else though, else he wouldn't have been able to cash in on people's urge for a "strong leadership".

He brags without inhibition (Lord Krishna would have disapproved), he calls himself "Son of India", he says those who preceded him were "against progress", and he has worn a coat in public that cost lakhs of rupees (betraying a deep-seated sense of anxiety behind the bold facade). These unusual attributes in the top leader were lapped up by the masses. They thought they had found their man. He seemed to attack the elites. They were certain he would look after their interests. But that time is now past.

Modi looks defeated when he takes the stage these days. He proffers jaded propaganda—such as farmers' incomes will double in five years; this at a time when more farmers are committing suicide every day across India than ever before. Also, when employment is rapidly shrinking.

No wonder Modi doesn't answer any questions, leave alone searching ones. He has no time for journalists, even less for his own MPs and ministers, who bow and scrape before him as before a sultan of yore, worried that they might be ejected from the gravy train otherwise.

External affairs minister Sushma Swaraj offered a typical example recently. At the UN General Assembly, she covered the routine on Pakistan being the home of terrorism, and then launched into fulsome praise of the PM for programmes such as Stand Up India and what have you, as she might at an election rally. "Good Luck India! Good Bye India!" One can almost hear that coming! Modi's India looks badly faded. It is divided and despairing.

In the three years Modi has been around as PM, he has used the state apparatus to intimidate opponents. In his name, thugs have let loose repression on Muslims, the dalit community (although the PM courts B.R. Ambedkar flagrantly, hoping to win dalit votes), poor tribal people, holders of contrary opinion, and intellectuals.

The return of state awards by prestigious writers, thinkers, artistes, and the hit-style murders of rationalists and dissenting journalists, inspired nationwide protests, but the *bhakts* or regime supporters are unfazed. Recep Tayyip Erdogan's Turkey has despatched opponents to jail. We are not there yet. But the age of fear is upon us, and the age of attacks on the nation's poorest. This takes us beyond authoritarianism—to a place from which quasi-fascism does not look so far.

The State's hungry beasts have been let loose on a particular television station, which in recent times has attempted to do straightforward, old-fashioned, journalism instead of keeling over like the rest and becoming a servitor of the regime. The Central Bureau of Investigation (CBI) is now a monster unchained. A former IAS officer and now a well-known activist for communal harmony, now touring the country with young people to spread the message of societal peace, is being threatened by the tax brutes.

As for the PM's ability to guide the country with sophistication and intellect (a requirement in a complex society like India), it will suffice to explore the contents of his "Mann Ki Baat" programme. There is no need to dissect crucial issues like demonetisation, GST, "surgical strike", Swachchh Bharat, Stand Up India, etc.

No wonder every economic metric points to a tired, shrinking economy with little hope of recovery in the foreseeable future. People are seething with discontent. The farmers are in revolt. The BJP's student wing, the ABVP, has lost university elections across India, although the important tests lie in Uttar Pradesh and Bihar. When the PM was in Varanasi, his constituency, last week, over 1,000 BHU women students protested life under the regime, including pointing to sexual violence, but Modi had no time for them. They were lathicharged. The friendly media looked the other way.

The PM and his cohorts give the call to protect India's honour and self-respect through militarism. Their way is to pay overt obeisance to the armed forces. The establishment speaks of placing tanks at university campuses to inculcate a healthy dose of patriotism among young people. Any day one expects ministers to arrive at cabinet meetings wearing jackboots and epaulettes. But can you honour the soldier when you dishonour the farmer? Isn't the jawan the "kisan in uniform"?

Small wonder then that the world is eager to hear Gandhi's message. People are paying attention partly because he put it across with remarkable ease—and pointed to truths that people already knew. After Berkeley, he highlighted rising unemployment and falling growth rates at Princeton, besides being substantive on India, China and the world.

RG is indeed discovering new territories. But there is a long way to go in channeling the discontent and building bridges with non-BJP parties, besides fixing his own badly suffering Congress.

Asian Age & The Deccan Chronicle, September 25, 2017

'Panels' in Praise of PM Modi at Gandhi's Sabarmati Ashram

As we take another step toward the 70th anniversary of our independence, and right after the distinctly 'Gandhian' means employed unsuccessfully by the BJP on the eve of the 75th anniversary of the Quit India Movement to win all the three Rajya Sabha seats from Gujarat, it is necessary to record the silent move of the Modi government a month ago to gatecrash Sabarmati Ashram, the Mahatma's *sanctum sanctorum*, in order to gild the PM's image.

If storming the electoral turf on the Ganga at Varanasi was done in public glare with energy and a rampaging will three years ago, Narendra Modi, now in the *avatara* of the Prime Minister, chose to insinuate himself into Mahatma Gandhi's ashram on the banks of the Sabarmati river in Ahmedabad, with practically no one noticing.

On a recent visit, this writer was shocked—and offended—on seeing at the famous ashram expensive looking panels singing paeans to Modi in the guise of lavishing praise on his government's trademark programmes which, experts believe, have fetched little by way of positive result for the country (in contrast with political dividend for his party and him personally) and, in short, constitute high-decibel propaganda.

Professionally mounted rare photographs on Gandhi's life with appropriate annotations in a series of rooms lead to an open verandah where the Modi panels stood. These were apt to give the impression to the uninitiated that the work being done by Modi is a natural extension of the Mahatma's experiments with truth, which the old photos endeavour to depict.

The photo-feature on the Mahatma's life and work continues outside the rooms, spilling over on to the verandah, not far from the Modi panels.

Indeed, the visuals on the Dandi March, the event that signalled breaking the salt law and infused momentum into the freedom movement at a difficult moment, are in the piazza, not in the rooms.

Seen in a critical spirit, this won't cut ice. But a large number of viewers, from the questions they asked of guides, appeared to be simple folk from different parts of the country likely to accept what they see, and what they are told, at face value.

Schoolgirl guides were posted in groups to explain the panels to enquiring visitors in the ashram museum block. They seemed to have been taught to give set, tutored, answers to easily anticipated questions. That made them parrot the official Modi propaganda.

Enquiries revealed that the media in Ahmedabad had not reported this invidious attempt of the government to encroach upon the Sabarmati Ashram which has been in its present location since 1917, although the institution was founded two years prior at a place nearby called Kochrab and had to be moved on account of the spread of plague in that village.

The Prime Minister was at Sabarmati in early July when a function was held to mark the centenary of the founding of Gandhi's ashram. Whether the installation of panels to highlight the Modi regime's programmes pre-dated this visit, or followed it. needs to be ascertained from the Sabarmati management.

The more fundamental question, of course, is who authorised the invasion of Gandhi's sanctum by the government's propaganda machinery a hundred years after the world-famous institution was founded. And what were the circumstances in which the decision was taken?

It is evident that the government converting an iconic national institution into a site of official propaganda may well have been intended to devalue the Sabarmati Ashram in the long run and dilute its appeal.

In ideological terms, Mahatma Gandhi is anathema to the RSS, from which Modi has risen, and to followers of the Hindutva ideology more broadly. It is they who assassinated him.

Journalist friends in Ahmedabad, when asked about how the BJP, the ruling party in Gujarat, views Gandhi now that it is in government, point to the example of the so-called "Mahatma Mandir" or temple in Gandhinagar, the state capital very near Ahmedabad. This Mandir is lavishly appointed. Tourist-guides conduct group tours. On display are facets of Gandhi's life. What's missing is the real story of his death. The name of Nathuram Godse is wholly absent. Welcome to BJP's Gandhi!

Maybe, it is this underlying spirit which informs the recent decision to mix the flavour of Gandhi's memory enshrined at Sabarmati with other, more mundane, things like governmental popaganda.

There may also be the Prime Minister's evident need to gain some legitimacy through Gandhi, and seek to broaden his appeal among those who do not hark back to the PM's ideological family. So far, the most important marker in Modi's biography is the 2002 Gujarat pogrom. But after transitioning to national leader, the emperor needs new clothes.

It's worthwhile asking if Modi could ever have qualified to be an inmate of Sabarmati Ashram. Eligibility rules were stringent, and enjoined on everyone daily physical labour and spartan living, not to mention celibacy. Changing your clothes to suit the occasion and to wear coats that cost lakhs of rupees was a disqualification. But Modi managed to muscle his way in, anyway.

Asian Age & The Deccan Chronicle, August 14, 2017

Nitish's Dodgy 'Total Revolution'

Bihar chief minister Nitish Kumar won the trust vote last Friday. But can he be trusted now?

The question is likely to haunt him all the way to the next assembly election in the state. That means three long years—a considerable length of time in which to be tormented by doubts and political and psychological uncertainties, and be dogged by the fear of being backstabbed by those he is depending on.

In such situations, people are known to fear their own shadow. Such a state of mind is unlikely to yield a coherent administration for Bihar. And in this time of witches and forests moving, as in Macbeth, he will have to continue plying his trade of being a quick-change artist. But a time comes when the protagonist finds the usual avenues blocked. As they say, when credibility is lost, everything is lost.

If the BJP wins the 2019 Lok Sabha election with a vengeance, and is able to repeat its parliamentary performance of 2014 in Bihar, then the countdown would have begun for Kumar. The saffron bloc in the state legislature may peremptorily cast him aside and threaten to withdraw support, compelling him to have a BJP CM replace him for the final year of the Assembly's term in order to better control the chessboard.

In that event, the next state election will be fought with a BJP CM in the saddle, just the objective that beckons the BJP-RSS. One possible way for Kumar to get out of the tangle may be to agree to don BJP colours and bury the Janata Dal (United), the party he founded.

The CM has now inextricably placed himself in a position

of servility to his saffron friends. Even the blind can see that the alliance he struck last week is on their terms, not his. Therefore, Kumar may reckon that his best interests may not be served with the BJP breasting the tape well ahead of the others in Bihar in the next Lok Sabha polls.

But wait. What if Lalu Prasad Yadav's Rashtriya Janata Dal, combining with the Congress and others, are able to hold the BJP in Bihar in 2019—a not entirely unimaginable prospect? In that event, the writing will be on the wall for the 2020 Assembly poll. The wholly opportunist decision to become a partner in BJP's sailboat could then begin to loom like a scary ghost for the "Chanakya" of Patna. The real Chanakya of Patliputra might have cautioned against the recent turnaround.

Another twist is also likely—that suddenly a large number of JD(U) MLAs profess a newfound love for the BJP. Demonetisation hasn't yet stripped horse-trading of its charms. The phenomenon of Opposition legislators finding unsuspected true love for Prime Minister Narendra Modi and Uttar Pradesh chief minister Yogi Adityanath has already surfaced in Gujarat and UP.

The BJP has fine-tuned the art of wholesale floor crossing of legislators in Arunachal Pradesh and Uttarakhand. Elections lost at the level of the people, have been won in the drawing rooms of governors. Goa and Manipur amply showed this.

The game is called snatching power from legitimate victors. Neither Modi nor "Kursi Chair" Kumar—the CM's new nickname denoting his love of office—view corruption in this, or they wouldn't be tweeting congratulations to one another. The devil is even citing scriptures.

The somersaulting CM now speaks of the mandate given to him to "develop" Bihar. He steadfastly refuses to acknowledge that the voters' mandate was given to him only after he joined Yadav's RJD and the Congress. It wasn't to stick to the BJP.

The Bihar CM cut his teeth in politics through the

Jayaprakash Narayan (JP) movement in Bihar in the early Seventies. But the "Total Revolution" that Kumar wrought in Patna last week, when he breathed new life into the defeated saffron brigade, mocks JP, the author of the concept.

It wasn't that JP was opposed to the RSS. The RSS, in fact, constituted the organisational backbone of his movement since there was no alternative machinery amongst his supporters. But that was a time when many—including obviously JP—thought of the Jan Sangh (BJP's predecessor)-RSS as committed ideologists, not Hindu-supremacists, powerbrokers and supreme wheelerdealers they are now widely seen to be, hammering the core of Indian nationalism and constitutional spirit.

JP had many sides in his long and distinguished ideological life—starting with Marxian affinities. He turned anti-Marxist along the way and eventually went over to Vinoba and Gandhi, whom he never abandoned even when he was being functionally solicitous of the RSS, who are the very antithesis of Gandhi.

In today's world, JP, without a doubt, would have given the saffron contingents short shrift. He was too much of a humanist not to recognise the "love jihad", "gau raksha", "ghar wapsi" and "surgical strike" brigades for being a kind of Hindu Al-Qaeda.

It is greatly interesting that his so-called shishya Nitish has returned to the bosom of the RSS, after leaving it (it appeared irrevocably), at a historical juncture when the BJP-RSS are power-drunk and breaking every convention of propriety.

For all his self-promotion in espousing ideals such as good governance and zero tolerance for corruption, Kumar is today getting to be seen in Bihar as the counterfeit article, not the real thing. It is clear that it is the BJP that has won the political round. The CM only lent them his shoulder to stand on. The celebrations in Bihar is at the BJP office, at the JD(U) headquarters only silence reins. People know the score.

It is clear as day that "Kursi" Kumar has been scheming

with Modi to topple his own government in Patna and to give the BJP a new lease of life in Bihar since September last year, when he came out all guns blazing in support of the socalled "surgical strike", which even sections of RSS sympathisers call " furjikal strike", playing on the Hindi expression " furji ", meaning false.

Still the CM says with a straight face that he ditched his own government in order to fight his deputy CM's corruption. Mr Kumar did not pause to consider that while the CBI has filed an FIR against Tejashwi Yadav, it is already prosecuting Union minister Uma Bharti in a criminal case, but the Prime Minister has neither resigned nor sought his minister's resignation on account of this.

Kumar let the BJP feed on his positive image built between 2005 and 2013, and allowed the saffron party to grow across Bihar. Then he dumped it. His calculation was that Modi's projection as PM, after the mass killing of Muslims in Gujarat, might cost him the Assembly election if he still stuck with the BJP. Now he sees that phase as being over, and has returned to his natural allies.

Asian Age & The Deccan Chronicle, July 31, 2017

Lessons from Gandhi that Modi could Learn

Narendra Modi took a lesson from his experience in London when he was last there as Prime Minister. So, in Washington recently, he flatly declined to take questions from the media. A joint press meet along with President Donald Trump was proposed by the American side and then taken off the menu.

Washington had suggested just one question each for the two leaders, not more. Evidently, the PM was keen to duck even that. He had been singed in London by a British reporter's volley on a Hindutva matter.

In Modi's India there are too many things happening simultaneously on the Hindutva front, and "Sabka saath, sabka vikas"—the anodyne mantra promising development for all without discrimination, as though this isn't what the Constitution mandates anyway—won't fob off a determined press in the Western hemisphere.

Frankly, it won't do so in India either. The Indian media has caved in by and large, scared further by bullying searches by the CBI, the Enforcement Directorate or income-tax authorities. But annoyingly for the government, the breed of questioning souls is not extinct in the press.

That's why the PM has taken to being blasé, not risking a single professional interaction with the community of journalists in three years, not even to repeat the tired taglines of his administration with which his one-way communication through the radio, television and social media—or when he takes the mike, specially in front of overseas Indians audiences—are plastered.

Like it or not, that's India's democratic dispensation for you at present. The star witness for the defence refuses to take the stand.

And in the current context, the killing of the 16-year-old Junaid Khan from Haryana by a Hindu lynch mob, who first accused him of being a "beef-eater" and then thrashed and knife-stabbed him to death before tossing his lifeless body on to a railway platform at a wayside station, was oven fresh when the PM landed in the US.

The boy was returning home from Delhi, where he'd gone for Id shopping. Id-ul-Fitr, the big day of Muslims, was three days away. The crime appeared too shocking, too brutal, too unreal to be true, and yet, the stark truth could not be hidden, not even by those who disabled the CCTV cameras.

The murder drew a gasp from anyone who heard about it, regardless of religious affiliation. But the Government of India heard nothing. Law minister Ravi Shankar Prasad was the exception. He alone responded with angered shock in a public statement, like a decent human being.

In his monthly radio broadcast "Mann ki Baat", aired on Sundays, Modi was cucumber cool. He pattered on about the sanctity of the Muslim fasting month of Ramzan, which culminates in Id. He praised a Muslim-majority village in Uttar Pradesh, which had built community toilets, spurning government funds. But on the cold-blooded murder of a young Muslim boy days before Id, he let maun vrat or silence prevail.

In this, he was being himself—one who sings paeans of self-praise and refers to opponents in indecorous and mocking terms, in season and out of season, within the country and when travelling abroad—and, studiously avoids making any mention of even deeply-disturbing happenings such as the killing of Muslims, the killing of dalits, the shooting dead of farmers by the police.

However, at Gandhi's Sabarmati Ashram on June 29, the

PM's hand was forced. The night before, in cities across India, including in the nation's capital, as well as at the renowned School of Oriental and African Studies in faraway London, ordinary Indians of many hues held massive protest rallies, calling these coordinated events "Not In My Name", to raise their voice against the lynching of Junaid and the rising tempo of mob killings of Indian Muslims in the name of cow protection.

Unofficial figures suggest there have been as many as 20 such episodes in the past six months alone, and there is no known record yet of anyone facing punishment.

At last Modi spoke at Gandhi's ashram, but was again anodyne. He said killings in the name of "gau bhakti" (cow-devotion) were "unacceptable", and "will not be tolerated". That's it. Nothing about what action would follow, or holding the authorities responsible.

Last August, the PM had called the vigilante killers "anti-social", giving us a new synonym for murder. The vigilantes are naturally unimpressed. Perhaps they know that Modi does not mean business and that threatening noises are pro forma.

The PM should ask himself a single question: "Is this how he would have reacted if members of the majority community had been targeted and done to death in cold blood by gangs roaming free"?

For good measure, Modi also said at Sabarmati Ashram that Gandhi would not have approved of what was happening and urged us to follow the Mahatma's teachings. Is this for real? If the PM means what he says, he will have to ask the RSS, the mother body of political Hinduism, to which he has paid allegiance since his teen years, to close shop. This is because the RSS and Gandhi are opposite poles, and those who assassinated Gandhi were influenced by the precepts of political Hinduism.

When the outrage of September 11 took place in America, the French gave the rallying cry, "Today we are all Americans!" This was a compelling expression of solidarity with the victims. It woke us up. If Gandhi were alive now, he would have gone on a fast, his hallmark act of atonement, and might have said, "We are all Muslims today!"

Can Modi understand that? Can his party? Can the RSS? The question is important because these entities are in power.

Just after the Partition of India, when communal hatred had made blood flow, Gandhi would rush to the aid of the Muslim and ask if he felt safe. Many Hindus did not like this. The Mahatma told them, if he were in Muslim-majority Pakistan he would have rushed to the Hindu and asked the same question.

Compassion for the victim was Gandhi's credo. This is also the essence of pluralism and democracy in the true sense. Modi does not seem to know this from his training or temperament. Can he still try to learn because he is the PM?

Asian Age & The Deccan Chronicle, July 3, 2017

India in 2017—Almost Orwellian

Many call it a "selfie" government, the chief protagonist clicking his own pictures, an act made easy by modern technology, in a project of driven self-projection—one day standing on a remote road in the far border region, another at the country's highest railway tunnel, in order to surreptitiously claim authorship of vital infrastructure projects that were more than halfway up before he arrived on the scene.

But such a description is casual; it is a serious under-representation of the reality of our times, of the period in which India is being turned into cuckoo land, of a day when people are being suckered.

They are being threatened by malevolent mobs and divided on lines of religion and caste, they are being impoverished but, for all that, they are led to believe that the authority on-high is their supreme benefactor—that he is on their side.

Through crafty speechifying, the poor are led to think Robin Hood has already robbed the rich to bring moneys to shower them with gifts. The rich—not just business and industry but also prosperous professionals—are being persuaded that market-oriented reforms have arrived and their businesses, indeed their country, will thrive, and go one notch up any moment.

Life has been contrived to make them live in hope. People haven't caught on that they are standing on one platform while the train is leaving from another.

They are still to figure out that the government which runs on acronyms—the latest being MODI, which is short for

Making of Developed India—is actually an advertising agency that sells images, cleverly-written lines effortlessly delivered, and dreams of postponed greatness, which demand sacrifices in the present to ensure that Big Brother can be made to stay put on the pedestal, otherwise all bets are off.

"It was a bright cold day in April, and the clocks were striking thirteen," wrote Eric Blair, better known as George Orwell, in *1984*. For us this is close to the bone. Those who live in India in the present day will instantly recognise their own everyday reality in this, a state of being which arises from the marked difference between what the government says and does, and what is.

The worship here is strictly of the *nirakaar*, the formless God. Those who sell the illusions know full well these will never take a concrete shape and form in the lives of the people. Wishes are not horses, and elephants will never fly. Quite simple.

We may be living in an India that is comprehensively Orwellian, and not know it. There is "doublespeak"—knowingly employing false play on words such as "surgical strike" to lull us into complacence that "the nation's enemies" have been dispatched—accompanied by the image of a conquering Lord Rama on stage in Lucknow with a bow and arrow, with the monkey-brigade dancing attendance.

And then there is "newspeak"— the high velocity propaganda (on television) carried out less by the official Doordarshan than the private channels falling at the feet of the government lest the Enforcement Directorate or the CBI come knocking on their door, as they do with leaders of the Opposition parties these days.

India has transmuted into a unique democracy where doublespeak and newspeak are the order of the day. It is a curious coincidence. *Nineteen Eighty-Four* took three years to write and was published in London on 8 June (of 1949). Right now, as we approach that very date, our rulers are in a celebration mode hyping up their three years in office—as though they had completed 30 years. Kim II Sung's successors do that sort of thing in North Korea—make a dark spot look bright, and through trickery make anything half-bright appear dazzling. Anyone you meet even in the BJP will agree, but on oath of secrecy.

Three years are a long time in politics. But the pall of immorality in public affairs and decrepit public ethics began to hang a long time ago, although no one was calling it out. The bubble could burst now, with the government's own data—recently released—showing quite convincingly that all this time we have been sold a dummy.

We are quite decidedly not the fastest growing large economy in the world, a claim that was growing tiresome with each passing day when each of us living in the real world knew this couldn't possibly be the case. The growth rate in the first three months of the present year—which captured the data right after the official end of demonetisation, undertaken to end black money—has shown how bankrupt the official policies have been.

The figures are the worst since the present lot assumed office. And if we take the "value added" figures—which is GDP tabulated in terms of goods and services made available—for the past year, then we have slipped to five per cent plus rate of growth for the economy, a steep fall of more than two per cent.

This is if we take 2011 as the base year, when the economy was in decline. This government did not wish to be judged by the yardstick of its predecessor and an earlier base year, which would have been more difficult to live up to.

Going by the earlier norm, the Narendra Modi government may have produced a growth rate below four per cent, exposing its dissimulation of three years and the use of Orwellian methods to supply a rosy, flimsy narrative.

In layman's terms, on account of faulty policies, jobs have been lost, capacities are languishing and businesses are not investing. Nor are they likely to in the foreseeable future, compounding the agony. The economy has shrunk. What's grown exponentially is cow vigilantism, exhortation of nationalism, loudspeakers declaring the Opposition parties corrupt and morally bankrupt, and militarist sabre-rattling because the government has no idea how to employ politics to seek a peaceful resolution of difficult issues.

If matters are not set right, we are staring at a political abyss, not just an economic one. The dalits are not impressed with the government kowtowing to win their votes through symbolic gestures like creating an "Ambedkar pilgrimage circuit", and are in rebellion. The Muslims are chafing. The backward Patels of Gujarat are on the warpath. This will happen when coercion is the mantra of governance.

Asian Age & The Deccan Chronicle, June 5, 2017

Is a 'Second Republic' Looming

What the decisive, compelling and devastating Narendra Modi victory in Uttar Pradesh has done is to pave the way for the inauguration of India's second republic. This signifies a historic departure from the value systems and mores of public life that flourished since 1950.

More, it green-lights the entrenchment of a new code of conduct, written or unwritten, in the running of the state and simultaneously offers official encouragement for the spread of the imagined social values of the Hindu majority that parade under the shorthand of "Hindu culture", an expression—given currency in recent decades—for which eminent Hindu religious scholars and experts are hard put to find cogent meaning.

In addition to this, there is a further angle that ties up with the promotion of "political Hinduism". This involves the manipulation of the system, specially the police and the judiciary, to condone extremist political actions of the kind that have been flagged as "Hindu terrorism", and scuttle trials in such cases, as we have seen the National Investigation Agency attempt to do in recent times.

Unlike the French case, when the country's Constitution was radically altered to usher in the present fifth republic (under Charles de Gaulle in 1958/59) in the crucible of Algerian decolonisation and weak parliamentary governments in metropolitan France, the second republic in India may just see a soft launch—no formal alterations to the basic structure (of being a democratic republic) for the time being, but a gradual ideological and political whittling down of the fundamental notions of an equal citizenship (and a reflection of this changed state of affairs in the daily life of the nation).

Since the inauguration of the Modi regime in 2014, a series of extraordinary "saffron-oriented" small violent eruptions have occurred, most frequently taking the form of 'cow-nationalism' and attacks on churches. These showed blatant disregard for the very notion of the rule of law and have occurred in all parts of the country, with the protagonists being generally associated with Hindutva outfits and victims being members of the minority communities or dalits.

There is no record of serious consequences being visited on the perpetrators, giving the impression of a quiet sanction being accorded to such a project from the side of the executive.

It needs to be said that Prime Minister Narendra Modi seldom fails to make the right noises. From a public forum he has sharply criticised the "gau-rakshak" vigilante brigades (the cow nationalists), calling them patrons of "gorakhdhandha " (irregular activity) and urged legal action against them.

However, it is striking that while the poor Muslim man Akhlaq was killed—in his Dadri home on Delhi's outskirts—on the false charge of keeping cow's meat in his kitchen, when a leader of the killer brigade died of the chikungunya illness shortly thereafter, the Hindutva outfits in the area held condolence meetings and received the public patronage of Union minister Mahesh Sharma.

Modi continued to tolerate this man in his council of ministers and expressed no displeasure. There is a clear feeling in saffron quarters by now that the PM's admonitions on the social front are meant just for the record and are not meant to be taken seriously.

As the PM, Modi enjoys enormous constitutional authority. Also, he is feared by BJP-RSS cadres across India and is held in awe by them after the stupendous election wins he has delivered. If the PM wants, he can put an end to law-breaking in any form and send Hindutva vigilantes running for cover.

But that is not his inclination, evidently.

In India, we are living in a historically-altered phase. This is not a matter of change of governments, a change of Prime Ministers, or the defeat of the Congress—the most coherent symbol of the "first republic"—and that party's long-term decline as a political machine.

It needs to be understood that the BJP, the political front of the RSS whose credo is "Hindu Rashtra" and not "democratic India", is a new type of party in our political system that has come to power in a dramatically impressive fashion—winning a massive majority in Parliament and in the country's largest state, besides controlling half a dozen other state governments.

This is a party which prides itself on projecting a religious ethos that is convenient only to the country's Hindu majority, and that is the feature that distinguishes it from all other parties in the country. In 1947, a post-colonial India emerged at the end of a longdrawn non-violent struggle in which all religious communities and caste and language groups of India were involved. To the RSS, this meant nothing.

The Hindutva parent outfit had shunned the national movement. In its eyes, the governments that came after the defeat of the British Raj were not "Hindu" governments as they did not privilege the country's Hindu majority. In its reckoning, the country's first Hindu government has come into being for the first time under the leadership of Modi.

This makes the present conjuncture a special moment for the RSS and the BJP. For them, a new dawn has broken. A dream of a Hindu Pakistan is today possible.

So long as the BJP has a comfortable majority in parliament and controls a large number of states, it does not need to show its hand and can carry on with the existing Constitution while making policy changes that enable the further rise of Hindutva as well as its entrenchment, e.g. through the educational system—just as they did in Pakistan under Gen. Zia-ul-Haq.

At the level of form, all would seem to be well even as the ideological and political erosion of the values of citizenship are made daily occurrences. Gandhi's portrait can continue to hang in the Prime Minister's Office room though his spirit would have long left it.

The only foreseeable problem for the saffron camp is that the entire edifice rests on one man. India's fundamental social structure and psychology has not changed, although there are rumblings at the margins, which made the rise of the BJP possible. As such, remove Modi from the equation and the BJP looks just as hollow or vulnerable as any other party.

In light of this, is 2019 already in the bag? Probably. But elections are a game that rest on social forces coming together or staying apart. The transition to the second republic cannot be completed if BJP's act comes unstuck in the next Lok Sabha election.

Asian Age & The Deccan Chronicle, April 10, 2017

Is Ram Mandir Next on the Agenda?

The Assembly elections in five states—whose results have sent the Opposition reeling—were really about Prime Minister Narendra Modi. The issue was whether he can win Uttar Pradesh, after BJP's crushing defeats in Delhi and Bihar. Given UP's heft in Indian politics, it was the only real prize to be won.

If, under Modi's leadership, the BJP had scored four on five, but lost UP, the hounds would be out in his own party first. That possibility, by no means remote before the state polls, is now history.

Everyone in the saffron fold, no matter how highly they may think of themselves, will now have no choice but to prostrate before the PM—and this includes the RSS hierarchy as well.

It is true Modi is the RSS' man who came good. His orientation is their orientation. He will do many things they will approve. But he will also, to make a point, overlook their claims and disregard their wishes.

After the stunning UP result showed who is boss, Modi will have to ensure everyone in the saffron fold understands only too well that they can't have expectations of him unless he desires them to do so. That is the unwritten law of power. The victory is Modi's, after all, not the BJP's.

About Atal Behari Vajpayee it used to be said that his strength in relation to the RSS lay in the fact that he was a RSS veteran of older vintage than even the RSS chief, and hence could afford to show the saffron caboodle down when he needed to. Modi will do this more often perhaps, not out of seniority but because he has earned more power from the voter on a consistent basis than any PM after Indira Gandhi, as India has lurched to the Right.

He doesn't any more need the RSS, they need him. And before long, he may be the one setting the who's who in the RSS top brass. Then, RSS will be the BJP by another name, and vice versa.

Top BJP leaders, although all have come through the RSS drill yard, are scared of the RSS and kowtow to it because they badly need its cadres to work for them at election time. Modi has now conquered that fear.

As UP has shown, within the space of less than three years, voters didn't flock to his side because the RSS cadre went about cooing a mantra in their ears. Voting is not a transcendental exercise in the end. All classes of people, and of all Hindu castes, turned out for this Gujarati whose Lok Sabha constituency lies in UP, because they perceive him as a no-nonsense "tough" leader who will fulfil their hopes.

It is true that Modi's "Mann Ki Baat" is trite. His speeches on the stump were seldom not a display of communal histrionics. His record of producing "development" for the poor masses of UP or of any state is shabby. Employment has been lost in the country. Prices of kitchen goods haven't settled down. But people are still ready to love Mr Modi.

Back in the day when the communications and propaganda revolution hadn't materialised, this might not have been the result. This factor has indeed helped the wily Modi hugely. But why hasn't it helped any other BJP leader, or any non-BJP leader?

The special attribute of the Prime Minister is that in the demographically young India, he can connect with the young- and the ill-educated but aspiration-seeking- Indian with surprising ease, blending semi-coarse asides with doses of nativism (not unlike Donald Trump), without pretensions of refined thought or sentiment. He leaves logic to the "secular", so-called "Harvard-educated" elite whom he scoffs at, and is loved by the crowds for that. He connects with them, they don't. And he sells them oodles of false consciousness.

Rahul Gandhi, for all his pedigree, tried to mock Modi, make fun of him, and ask daily questions. He had no narrative of his own that he could convey to the people in a language they understand. He chose to bat on Modi's bouncy track and was frequently hit wicket. The rest of the centrist and Left crowd chose not to bat at all.

The last three years in particular have seen Opposition politics at its most bankrupt. At a time when the star of the Hindu Right was in the ascendant, these self-proclaimed legatees of Marx, Gandhi, Nehru and Lohia had nothing to say for themselves. Their parties existed exclusively as rickety election-fighting forums, not as dynamic platforms of mass politics in a democracy.

The Congress has coarsened its language without mastering that particular craft pioneered by Mr Modi, and studiously not elaborated on the change it wants or ways to bring it about. Small wonder it has done far worse on the political and electoral landscape of late than, say, the Democrats have in the United States.

The latter had clear, well-articulated, ideas on the principal issues, and able leaders to put these across. The Congress' leadership's style, on the other hand, is to mistake two or three-liners for the full rendering of a narrative. Things have gone very, very wrong and it's time the Congress Party expected a run on the bank. The "bombing of the headquarters" may be said to be imminent, promoting palace intrigue.

As for the Left, the less said the better. Its leaders have forgotten the art of mass politics and mastered the dubious technique of long-winded statements that say little. Even when the country was hit by demonetisation and the poorest Indians suffered the most as a consequence, the Left was conspicuous by its silence. It also goes missing when communal violence is unleashed. It shows neither diligence nor flair.

Modi has finessed inner-party politics and bested the RSS. He has routed centrist forces and the Left. He should thus have everything going for him. But does he? His economics and his politics have so far revealed nothing that can bring "development" for ordinary Indians. He will probably carry on being all talk and no action. To get out of the jam, he may just about launch the building of the Ram Mandir in Ayodhya. Don't be surprised. We may all then say "Hey Ram!"

Asian Age & The Deccan Chronicle, March 13, 2017

PM Doesn't Know it, The Joke's On Us

In the present election season, as a fifth of the country considers what works for it and what doesn't, we should remember that it was only two and a half years ago that the country witnessed a sweeping wave of "Modi love", even a Modi-mania. This was why the party of the present Prime Minister was able to produce a first clear majority in the Lok Sabha in a quarter century on the strength of a mere 31 per cent of the vote.

This had shocked purists and critics of the BJP. But this was evidence that the Modi-wave was concentrated. Ordinary people were out in astonishing numbers to vote in the guy they wanted. They thought—very wrongly, it turns out—that he would be the answer to their prayers, that he would take them to shore. The election had been made American-style presidential in style through Narendra Modi's tactical cleverness, and he triumphed—and how.

A very different mood has settled on the country since then. Modi's buzz words have produced mostly vapour though they go by energising names such as "surgical strike" and "demonetisation" as he dons his hat, brimming with "nationalist pride", and goes dancing to places like Madison Square Garden in New York.

The words made commonplace by Modi have produced no dividend for the people. Go ask the farmers. Ask the workers, in agriculture and in cities. Ask the businessman and the industrialist—big or small. But most of all, ask the unemployed, whose lines have grown, not shortened.

Ask not just the students but also their parents, whatever

their caste, class, religion or region. You may wonder where love has gone—in such a short space of time.

On the one hand, there are these days the PM's "Mann ki Baat". It comes down like hard rain one Sunday every month. On the other, there is the government's own data. In spirit, the two are not in accord—they suggest very different things. The first tries hard to ignite hope, the second shows the PM the mirror.

But Modi is not fazed. It is a poor joke on the country when he repeats at the drop of the RSS cap that we are the world's fastest growing major economy. However, to achieve this we have changed definitions and the way the national income is calculated. And we refer to a time when world petroleum prices were at a historical low. But now they are climbing, and there has been demonetisation, to make matters worse. But those in authority patter on.

The people are tiring of these games. It is time one of the two stopped. Either the Sunday sermon should be switched off by DD and AIR or the government should end the colonial-era practice of publishing official data. This is easily done. All it needs is a rousing speech invoking nationalism or patriotism and the customary reference to two greats—Swami Vivekananda and Sardar Patel, besides *Manu Smriti* and the *Samahitas*.

If parliament insists on seeing the information to be able to judge the government's performance in line with its constitutional mandate, let the government offer sheer propaganda—data so tweaked and on such a massive scale as to become "alternative facts" of the kind that may encourage even US President Donald Trump's hard-boiled advisers to turn to New Delhi for advice.

All this belongs to the higher realms. To the ordinary Indian, the pitch of life in India has been on a disheartening descent path since Mr Modi's arrival on the scene. This can hardly be a surprise as the PM himself appears determined to lower the tone each time he wades into public territory through his speeches or his Twitter account, and those who differ with him are lampooned, blackmailed and threatened.

Major elections have not been won as a result, however. But the burning rage under Modi's monogrammed coat that cost rupees 10 lakhs (too bad it is in a museum now) has led the PM to practically call his predecessor corrupt on the floor of parliament through the analogy of the raincoat man. The deep complexes Modi appears to harbour have made him call Rahul Gandhi names that hardly redound to the credit of the PM of India. We have hit the level of the street.

What this "chai-khana" raucousness brings in Uttar Pradesh is of course unknown, but the feedback from Modi's own party and the RSS can hardly elate him. Manmohan Singh and Gandhi should not lose heart. All they need to do is consult their colleagues in the upper echelons of the BJP to know the mood in the saffron camp. It is not very different from the one in the Congress and the country. The Modi "fatigue" has spread.

The PM's colleagues are getting tired of having to lower their gaze if they must speak in cabinet meetings. Some throw up their hands in despair. Everyone is hoping that BJP president Amit Shah, fetched to the scene by Modi to manage the party for him but no one's favourite, goes back to Gujarat. But deliverance can only come from a certain kind of result in UP. The BJP's first rung is praying for deliverance. The second rung too. Ditto the farmers and the workers.

A good result for them may brighten their mood. But the country will take time to recover. The story so far is that every word spoken from on high and the major policies undertaken have been a cruel joke on the people. "Achche din" and the promise of rupees 15 lakhs in everyone's bank account from the black wealth recouped cause amusement, but sheathe a frustration. "Demonetisation" and "surgical strike" bring on derision. "Swachh Bharat" causes a guffaw.

It is no secret that our institutions are being eroded. The Reserve Bank of India (RBI) was asked to sign on the dotted line on demonetisation, leaving a stain on the autonomy of the country's monetary authority. A few months ago, the PM told a meeting of the country's top judges, presided over by the Chief Justice of India, that cases were piling up in courts because judges took holidays and didn't work hard. Unworthy individuals have been appointed at valued institutions like the IITs, JNU, ICHR and Nalanda University to advance dubious causes. But the PM still thinks that India is winning.

Asian Age & The Deccan Chronicle, February 13, 2017

The Big 'D' & Links with Big 'E'

Demonetisation has been such a resounding disaster for the people and the country that the term is likely to enter our political lexicon with a capital "D", much like "E" for Emergency. The difference between the two episodes is, however, stark.

Barring a clutch of the so-called "Young Turks", an energetic but minor woolly socialism-oriented faction in the Congress, Prime Minister Indira Gandhi's party stuck by her through the Emergency, although it was becoming plain, as the days wore on, that this method of fighting political opponents was going to boomerang badly. Prime Minister Narendra Modi is not so blessed.

His Demonetisation is being likened to the Emergency in that it has taken away the liberty of the people to work by creating such a devastating condition of absence of cash that the hirer is deterred from offering daily-wage employment, although there is work to be done.

The list of other negatives is long and well-known, and is reminiscent of the Great Depression of the 1930s, though we are not quite there yet. People are finding it difficult to buy food even if they have some money in the bank as they can't withdraw their own money.

Their everyday miseries are being compounded in a variety of ways, and the prospect of the economy regaining its verve in the foreseeable future seems not even a distant possibility at the moment.

This is why the BJP's MPs and MLAs, specially from poll-bound states like UP and Punjab, are deeply disturbed. They've anyway been unhappy for long as the Modi government has done so little for the farming community. The RSS, which makes or breaks BJP leaders, is said to be dissatisfied. Although its top brass have shown restraint in their speech, they know India has been struck a body blow by Demonetisation.

A vastly experienced outfit like the RSS can see the writing on the wall. In conditions like these, it is likely to be exploring fallback options to prepare for a scenario in which the Modi motif has been taken off the shelf.

Unlike the case of the Emergency, senior people in the Modi government and the BJP are not ready to speak up in defence of Demonetisation. In private, they roundly condemn it, and deeply worry for their political future.

Those in the BJP and the government who are speaking up for Demonetisation can be counted on the fingers of one hand, but are principally just two—finance minister Arun Jaitley and BJP president Amit Shah who, along with PM Modi, make up the trio that are running the show, as was derisively pointed out by Arun Shourie, a writer and former journalist who commanded much respect in the (Atal Behari) Vajpayee period.

But even Jaitley and Shah are careful how they put across their thoughts. The finance minister has indeed found a clever way. He speaks *ad nauseam* about digital cash and plastic money but remains completely quiet about how to address the bread and butter issues of the people.

The BJP president, on the other hand, has the image of a bully. He inspires fear, not affection; he tells his party ranks to take the message of the government to the people instead of complaining and malingering. But he is careful not to elaborate his thoughts on the positive features of Demonetisation. His party colleagues tend to give him a wide berth. But when confronted by him they dare not contradict him to his face, and prefer to stay mum.

In short, the people are deriving the message of

Demonetisation through their own experience, not through the channels of the party machinery or the widespread RSS network. Initially, many among the poorer classes did appear to be satisfied. They grew vicarious pleasure—and solace—from the thought that Demonetisation was intended to be a blow struck at the heart of the fatcat, and of big business. Now people know better.

It wasn't just that the banks were denying the public their own hard-earned cash while they were stealthily serving their high-end customers. Enough indications are now becoming available to suggest that clever tricks to favour the rich start not at banks but at the government security presses, where new currency notes are being printed—for example, wads of fresh notes of the Rs 2,000 denomination are marked as wads of Rs 10 notes and spirited out.

The thought is inescapable that Demonetisation was a political move, not a well-considered economic one (or it would have been much more expertly handled). It aimed to excite the poor man's inner anger with the rich and leave behind the subliminal thought that Prime Minister Modi was on their side and intended to get even with the rich on their behalf.

Indeed, it was planned as a gigantic PR exercise to boost Modi's image with ordinary people for the purpose of gaining their confidence, first for the Uttar Pradesh and Punjab polls in February, 2017 and then the Lok Sabha poll of 2019, since the government's track record is otherwise thin.

In this respect, it was like the "surgical strike", which turned out to have no military value but it did catch the public imagination initially. But the hoax has now been found out. How will the poor behave? Shakespeare cautioned us long ago: "Beware the fury of a patient man!"

Modi must have been made more aware of this last Friday when he addressed the BJP Parliamentary Party. Images of the event on television showed there was a sullen silence. The Prime Minister himself looked haggard and distraught, not his usual confident, crack-the-whip self. He pulled out scrappy lines from a book written by a long-ago bureaucrat to condemn Indira Gandhi and quoted from sundry speeches of Indira-baiters to slam her.

But his audience remained unmoved. The Prince of Gujarat was walking the razor's edge and his feet were bleeding. But those who saw him thus seemed to feel no pity.

With a mood such as this within the BJP, how could Modi have summoned the nerve to allow a proper discussion on Demonetisation in Parliament? And not inviting a debate on the most important economic policy measure in decades is a scornful rejection of the democratic process.

Asian Age & The Deccan Chronicle, January 27, 2017

It is Important to Keep Asking Questions

I found myself in Kashmir last week, along with friends, speaking to scores of young people, many of them well-educated young professionals—lawyers, doctors, teachers, journalists. There's no way to know, but some among them may have been associated with stone-pelting in order to vent their anger, or as a conscious decision to register a political sentiment which is emblematic of the times.

Since dialogue has become a dirty word in New Delhi, the Kashmiris have been engaging in ferocious monologue. It's another matter we think they will come to their senses sooner or later and the strategy seems to be to let them stew. The consequences can be unpleasant of course. But just listen to the snatches of one conversation:

"You call us secessionists. Military force is unleashed against us. We are being blinded. Pellet-guns are being used even against children. We are anti-national. Today Ghulam Nabi Azad (a former chief minister of J&K) was called anti-national. This happened in the Indian Parliament. And he is the Leader of the Opposition. Thank you, Indian democracy."

So cynical was the tone, the speaker may as well have added "Good-bye, Indian democracy!"

It was shaming to hear.

"Anti-national" has suddenly become the new normal. It can be said of anybody, anywhere, any time. The expression seems to have lost its original meaning. Now it simply means, anyone who differs with me is an "anti-national" (provided

BJP is on my side).

It's a curse word sanctioned by frequent usage by high functionaries of the ruling establishment. It's as though our political popes have set up an invisible court which punishes without trial and barks out as punishment that curt, accusative, word with an ominous ring.

Why ominous? Because if you are "anti-national", you can be hit by any roadside goon, no questions asked. A dog is given a bad name and then beaten. This is a sure way to descend into the stairwell of darkness, but the bailiffs of the invisible court beam with righteous pride.

Today is their day. Awarding certificates has become their right. Only they have earned the moral sanction to guard the nation.

This is exactly as the Pakistan army thinks of itself as it sends its opponents to the dungeons delineated in Mohammed Hanif's *A Case of Exploding Mangoes*. We are not yet at the base camp of fascism, but that destination is not so dimmed in the mist.

The media has fallen in line. Prominent television stations have been intimidated and the others are doing the needful. The newspapers have held out on the whole, but just about. They tread with caution. They spill out the propaganda on their front pages, and ask few questions.

An even better technique is to unfailingly show the government's opponents in poor light and ask no questions of government policy or its execution.

The top judges are still standing up to the poisoned darts being shot at them, but no one knows for how long. Parliament can be our best hope yet, but our representatives have still to demonstrate that they are capable of innovating. Walkouts are not the only way to show challenge to untrammelled authority. In fact, in India that has become an exhausted channel, an unthinking one that leaves people unimpressed.

Before they leave the chamber in disgust, our elected representatives are expected to put up a fight by offering painstaking resistance and careful arguments so that the time of the House is not seen as going waste.

Carefully picking out questions to ask is a necessary aspect of life in Parliament to keep the executive on its toes. In our own day, when "anti-national" is being raised to the level of a phonetic meme of the Far Right to cover its tracks for failing to live up to its many promises to ordinary people, it is important to ask the rulers if they have been scrupulous about observing the sanctity of institutions and respecting their delineated boundaries.

Two "surgical strikes" have been carried out lately. One concerns the Army. That expression was officially used—and publicised—to describe a cross-LoC (Line of Control with Pakistan) raid in late September against tin-sheds in PoK (Pakistan-Occupied Kashmir) where terrorists gather before they are sprung into Indian territory by their Pakistani handlers.

The other relates to the Reserve Bank of India, the custodian of monetary activity in the country, in the context of the government's decision to declare certain high denomination currency notes useless.

This was not officially described as a "surgical strike" against black money, but leading lights of the ruling party have used that description liberally in an effort to impress voters.

In both cases, there can arise reasonable doubt that the domains of the institution of the army and that of the RBI were encroached upon by the government, and they were not asked to or permitted to supply their professional input in decision-making—that they were railroaded and bulldozed.

Was the army asked if "surgical strike" was the appropriate expression for its raid on the night of September 28? It is necessary to know because the flashy and exalted use of that high-profile term in the present context can only have had a specific pre-election purpose (for the upcoming assembly election in politically-sensitive Uttar Pradesh).

In short, the Army was dragged into a political manoeuvre; the executive obliged it to acquiesce in the patently false use of that military description with a precise meaning.

The implication is that politics was made to breach the professional preserve of the army, and the top boys caved in. This is an eerie sign of system erosion. A satisfactory explanation of what transpired is owed to Parliament.

In the case of demonetisation, the other "surgical strike", the implementation has been so shockingly shabby as to suggest that it was not thought through at all and was a pre-election gambit of doubtful public worth.

In that event, questions may be raised if the professional view of the RBI was sought, or whether the monetary authority was simply asked to sign on the dotted line in disregard of the rules of the game.

Both questions concern the preserving of institutional integrity within the system. In the case of both, the disgraceful epithet of "anti-national" has been hurled at individuals for either pointing out shortcomings or raising doubts. Parliament, the shop-floor of democracy, has a right to be informed.

Asian Age & The Deccan Chronicle, November 21, 2016

Surgical Strike—What was it Really?

It is hard not to recall the great relief the country felt when news came around September 29 mid-day that the Indian Army had sent its commandos across the Line of Control (LoC) to take out "launchpads" where terrorists had been assembled for crossing over into Kashmir.

This relief was mingled with some pride in our army. But a month down the line, troubling questions arise. Therefore, the question is: if there were no election, and one as crucial as UP, would there have been a "surgical strike"?

Just about everything that has happened since the cross-LoC raid points that way. Ram and Ravan hoardings were put up by the BJP all across UP, with Prime Minister Narendra Modi portrayed as Ram and Pakistan PM Nawaz Sharif as Ravan. Breaking from tradition, Modi, as PM, made his Ramlila address not from the nation's capital but in Lucknow, the capital of UP, where the crucial polls are due.

He didn't say a word about the September 29 strike in his speech, but took up from the stage the slogan "Jai Shri Ram; Jai, Jai Shri Ram!", a Hindu battle cry and the RSS' and BJP's mobilising motif before the destruction of the Babri Masjid in December 1992. (In Hindi, the chant of the devotee—unlike the strident cry—is: "Siyawar Ramchandra ki Jai".)

The meaning was not lost on anyone. It seemed clear that Modi was going for broke, leaving nothing to chance, and the military action was to be handily exploited.

Defence minister Manohar Parrikar made his own egregious—and false and communal—contribution. He first said it was the BJP government that had made the army realise its strength. This was an insult to the army. At another forum he noted it was the RSS training that Modi and he had which made the "surgical strike" happen. This gave the army's action a communal colour. Not a word from the defence minister about the army's quietly stellar role that night. And to rub the point in, the defence minister falsely averred that cross-LoC action had not been done before by the army, as if "Operation Ginger"—larger in scale than the September 29 action—of the Manmohan Singh years didn't exist.

How refreshingly different things were after the Kargil conflict. With an unerring eye for low-grade publicity, the BJP put up hoardings with the images of our armed forces chiefs. Gen. V.P. Malik, the then Army Chief, informs us that he told Prime Minister Atal Behari Vajpayee that this amounted to politicising the military. The propaganda material was promptly withdrawn.

After the massive military victory over Pakistan in 1971, which led to the creation of Bangladesh, the Indira Gandhi government did not put up any credit-grabbing posters. In fact, it was the Jan Sangh (BJP's precursor) leader in Parliament then, none other than Vajpayee, who hailed Indira as "Durga".

We must ask Lt. Gen. Ranbir Singh, director-general of military operations, a question that he must ponder before answering: Where did the expression "surgical strike", that he used while breaking the news of September 29 to the country, come from?

Was it a suggestion from political or bureaucratic quarters? Or did the Army really think that what had been achieved was indeed a surgical strike, an evocative and seductive term that bespeaks spectacular military prowess and lends itself to political misuse. The question is pertinent as this expression has never been used by our armed forces before. Also, the operation carried out in the small hours of September 29 was not a surgical strike by any accepted military definition.

At the very least, a surgical strike stuns and incapacitates the adversary for a while. But nothing of the sort happened. A string of army camps was attacked by terrorists in J&K within days of September 29. Lt. Gen. Satish Dua, head of the Srinagar-based 15 Corps, had observed last week that terrorists were massed in strength on the LoC "in spite of the surgical strike", preparing to infiltrate.

The field manual of the US Special Forces derives the meaning of "surgical strike" from the Army Doctrine Publication ADP3-05 (Special Operations), and this is the prevalent internationally followed definition, including in India. According to it, a surgical strike is a "primarily unilateral application of force" (while ours came in response to a succession of terrorist attacks, culminating in Uri) employed in counter-terrorism... against designated targets, and other specialised tasks of strategic importance". "High payoff targets" are to be hit. A surgical strike "shapes" the environment, and is used to "degrade effectiveness of adversaries".

Which of these objectives was achieved on September 29? The "launchpads" destroyed were little more than cowsheds. If a "surgical strike" is devalued to mean any successful commando strike, then what the Pakistani terrorists attained at Uri might also qualify. Is that the equivalence we are looking for?

Asian Age & The Deccan Chronicle, October 24, 2016

Craven Journalism at Its Worst

Lal Bahadur Shastri's slogan at the time of the 1965 war with Pakistan, which echoes to this day, was "Jai Jawan, Jai Kisan". Our then prime minister understood that the brave jawan could stand tall because the doughty kisan stood guard behind him- with food supplies that fuelled the nation's economy.

Shastri was careful not to leave out the "kisan" even when a war was on.

But PM Modi is different. He seems happy with just "Jai Jawan!" This is consistent with how little has been done for the poor kisan in his regime, though there have been words galore. But chiefly, he thinks this will make him look "strong".

No, we are not near a Fourth Reich yet. But Third Reich thought - of looking "strong", saluting the soldier at the drop of a hat, asking no questions of a department of the government called the army, and becoming "nationalistic" by hurling the expletive of "anti-national" or "traitor" at everyone outside your fold- is upon us.

In fact, this is a catching disease and the first to have caught it are prominent sections of the television media who have converted themselves into nationalistic media warriors.

After the "surgical strike", some sat in their studios reading the news and conducting discussions wearing military-style flak jackets, mimicking soldiers. Poor chaps. Their mission was not to cross the LOC or do cross-border reporting. That needs gumption.

They just wanted to win the *studio-vir chakra* by pleasing the PM and the ruling party, and chalk up favours or lodge a credit so that the government may have no cause to look into any irregularities they may have been guilty of in the past.

Quid pro quo is the name of the game. Saving your skin is the name of the game. And they are all winning the game of being craven. One channel typified what's going on. It said the PM's speech in Lucknow on the day of Vijayadashmi this year, staged in the first place to extract political mileage for the cross-border raid of September 29 before the UP Assembly election, was a "surgical strike on the opposition". Just imagine what might have happened if a war had been won, like in 1971.

PM Modi and his party love the jawan because our soldier is a silent hero. He doesn't "reason why". He is "ready to do and die", just like in the lines of Tennyson's famous poem.

The soldier will stand stiffly to attention even if the politician jumps onto his back and stands up on his shoulders to take the salute. You can't do this with the kisan. The fellow will gather his tribe and march to Parliament House, denouncing the government all the way.

To a politician, the kisan is a tricky customer; therefore, he is no use. The jawan is the opposite. When it comes to "nationalism", it is the politician in India who speaks the loudest, and the trooper lets him. He goes about his business quietly- not bothered with accolades.

This was summed up graphically in a newspaper cartoon recently which contrasted the situation in neighbouring countries. In Pakistan, the cartoon showed, the Army was the Naked Ape that had climbed on top of the politician, while in India the Naked Ape was the politician who had climbed on top of the soldier.

This is regretfully our reality. But the media is not saying so. The brilliant political cartoon is the dazzling exception. What's going on otherwise is stiff competition in the media to demonise the opposition while seeking to notch an entry into the good books of the ruling party.

It is hard to recall another time like this in India. In the

Emergency years, the ruler was extolled but the opposition was not punched around in the media and called names, leave alone on a steady basis.

A particular channel has gained particular notoriety since the Modi sarkar was ushered in. Studio guests on the carefully prepared list go on a hunt each day, led by the especially obnoxious anchor. They lynch that one guest who is not on the government's side. The show has got nauseating by now. But people seem to like gladiator sport, whatever they may choose to do at the hustings- as we saw in the Delhi election and then in Bihar.

A rival channel- a "sober" one, which claims to give us news, not noise- has now joined the ranks of the faithful. A few days ago, it interviewed P. Chidambaram, who was finance minister in the last government and before that the country's home minister- in both capacities a member of the Cabinet Committee on Security.

Chidambaram has publicly asked some leading questions about the "surgical strike". Probably that's why the interview was conducted in the first place. This showed good professional news sense. Extracts from the interview were run on the network to whet appetite. But the interview vanished into thin air. It was not shown. Period.

There were no explanations to the viewer. It would be a reporting coup of sorts if an enterprising journalist can land the story one day what happened behind the scenes. Was there threat held out by the government? Or, was there temptation? Or, a jumble of the two?

In lieu of the viewers getting the Chidambaram interview, an internal communication in the channel informed all concerned that they worked for a serious news organisation which believed in standing by the country's armed forces and would not countenance anyone politicising the actions of the army.

Many journalists who work for this outfit now revealed to be weak-kneed and shabby, almost all in fact, felt personally humiliated by this Orwellian talk. The reason is that the ruling party chaps are having a field day on the same channel as they milk the "surgical strike" dry for politics. How the mighty have fallen.

Are individual journalists on the take? Is that the reason why the PM and his party are getting a free pass? The thought is absurd, although a few bad apples can always be found. The problem is more structural, really.

A number of news outlets these days are run by businessmen or politicians with a close nexus with the saffron party that is running the show. And that's the story. The Indian media today, or prominent sections of it in any case, arguably represents the worst in journalism for any democracy- being the least hard working, the least enlightening, the least questioning.

Pakistan is no democracy. It's also had the tradition of "Trust papers and Trusted papers", which cannot do any country credit. But elements of the Pakistan press are top-notch. This is because they dare to hold the mirror to their rulers.

The Citizen, October 16, 2016

Vajpayee, Manmohan Singh and Now PM Modi: The Naughty Bee Stings Again

A basic issue that undercut former Prime Minister Atal Behari Vajpayee's re-election bid in 2004 and showed up the hollowness of his "India Shining" campaign was a sustained period of jobless growth.

Although other factors contributed, a lacklustre jobs front decisively turned the mood of the electorate against the government of Dr. Manmohan Singh although it had delivered an average growth of an unprecedented seven per cent per annum over a 10-year period, not achieved under any democratic dispensation in the world.

Now it seems Prime Minister Narendra Modi's turn to be stung by the same naughty bee. Not creating jobs can scuttle communal projects of his party to rake in the Hindu vote through the much-glorified nationalism route. It is this-and of course the stubbornly high prices of everyday essentials such as dal which refuse to subside—which is emerging as the crucial political factor in the upcoming Assembly election in UP expected in just about six months' time- and the BJP is showing signs of running scared.

In a laboured 90-minute address from the Red Fort on Independence Day, the Prime Minister cited a jumble of data to show that his government excelled in the difficult art of implementation, and concentrated on "making the impossible possible".

Recounting his "achievements", the poor man in his desperation even listed the release of the Subhash Bose papers from the archives as a singular achievement, although the published material has left no one any the wiser about whether "Netaji" had indeed died or still lives amongst us disguised as a sadhu baba (mendicant). But doer-man Modi was careful to offer no data concerning the employment scene, noting only that if small businesses prospered, and shops kept open longer hours, they could hire more people.

This was noticed even by a panel of high-profile analysts- who revealed themselves to be diehard Modi devotees- in a post-speech television discussion. The grey-beards noted with marked reluctance that the Prime Minister should have referred to the issue of unemployment, and proffered plans to address the crucial issue. The big dodge brought beads of perspiration to their brow.

At the Red Fort grounds itself, people didn't show signs of being particularly enthused with the speech. Leave alone the "Modi, Modi" cries of approbation that were frequent at the PM's rallies earlier, on this occasion it is hard to remember if the crowd even clapped.

This is because everyone knows what the score is. The writing is on the wall. Being more perspicacious that others in the saffron camp about matters "political" (rather than "cultural"), the RSS has known for some time that there is little hope of righting the employment situation so long as extreme pro-market foreign prescriptions continue to obsess the Modi regime.

And being a fairly alert outfit, the RSS has launched heavy-duty propaganda across the country. Under this line of falsity being spread, the hope is being held out to the poor that although the Modi sarkar has belied its election promises and given them nothing so far, it will give them much in the future.

The argument goes that such important and spectacular plans have been set in motion for the benefit of ordinary people that these can bear fruit only in three or four years' time. "Does a tiny plant become a giant tree in one day?" the people are asked.

The line can be heard in all parts of the country. And an appeal to elect Modi in 2019 inevitably follows- so that he may give you in future what he couldn't now. The message to the needy is: "A bird in the bush is worth two in the hand." It is difficult to think of greater political chicanery.

Of course, no one is buying the lollipop. The "goli"- the colourful expression commonly heard in the north to denote a trickster's lie- is just not selling, and people are chafing at the bit. As the Lohiaites used to say, "Zinda qaumein paanch saal intezar nahin kar saktin." (People who are alive can't wait five years!)

Signs of this could be seen in Varanasi earlier this month when lakhs of people flocked to Congress leader Sonia Gandhi's rally right in the heart of Modi's Lok Sabha constituency. Earlier, party vice-president Rahul Gandhi had received a very warm response at an event in Lucknow.

It is commonly thought that the election result in UP will either shut the door in Modi's face, or cheer him on to another triumph in 2019. It is early to make predictions, but signs of anxiety are visible in BJP-RSS circles.

The saffronites had hoped to carry on from the momentum of the 2014 Lok Sabha election in which BJP claimed 71 of the 80 seats in UP, retain the affections of the upper caste, maintain a hold over the non-Yadav OBC and the non-Jatav dalit voter.

This calculation seems to be going awry with a string of attacks on dalits by the Hindutva fanatics "gau-rakshak" or cow-protection platoons across the country, the most notable being the one at Una in Gujarat in July. The upper caste Brahmins and Rajputs are also showing signs of veering away from the BJP, as they see some signs of a Congress revival.

When the situation is looking anything but comfortable, a diktat of BJP chief Amit Shah to his party MPs in UP is making these worthies run for cover. Shah has ordained that every MP should aim to ensure wins for the BJP in at least three Assembly segments of his parliamentary constituency. For their part, the MPs believe that Shah is losing touch with the ground reality.

They say that the economic scene is so grim in Modi's raj- with runaway prices and no jobs- that they dare not show their faces to those who voted for them. "Where is then the question of making the BJP win on three Assembly seats in my constituency?" is a common refrain.

What this foretells can only be guessed at. But the RSS is doing what it can to shore up the regime by raising the cry of hyper-nationalism to combat ghosts that threaten to emerge from a poor man's empty kitchen. Its chief Mohan Bhagwat himself jumped into the fray in Agra last week. He asserted that "Hindutva equals nationalism", and urged Hindus to have children in much greater numbers. If this goes viral, BJP's political opponents could have a field day.

The Citizen, August 24, 2016

No Place for the Opposition Here

When Parliament House was assaulted by terrorists some 15 years ago and Prime Minister Atal Behari Vajpayee was trapped inside, the first call he received—enquiring with urgency if he was all right—was from Congress leader Sonia Gandhi.

Vajpayee revealed this in a stirring speech in the Lok Sabha shortly afterward. And he made it a point to emphasise that democracy was safe in a land in which the Leader of the Opposition was full of concern for the leader of the government.

Alas, we have slipped so comprehensively from that era. And it is unlikely to be anyone's case that the situation is retrievable—at least not until the present lot stick around. And if Vajpayee's assertion about democracy holds water, then it is plain that our system is being shaken to its roots by those in authority. Democracy is being administered electric shocks. Nothing lasts forever, of course, but that is another matter.

The record of the past two years suggests that this government's principal purposes are not related to governing. Its well-crafted failure to reach working consensus in parliament to get important measures through, and the near abrogation of its responsibility to deal with the drought gripping 40 per cent of the country, testify to its indifference to the cause of governance. Examples can be multiplied.

Instead, it seems the first object of the Modi government is to hound the Opposition and go for its jugular, and have its leading lights thrown into prison if possible—starting with

Sonia and Rahul Gandhi. Perhaps the calculation is that if the Gandhis can be put out of business, then the Congress Party would be put out of business.

That is Rashtriya Swayamsevak Sangh's (and Bharatiya Janata Party's, of course) final frontier, its most cherished dream. As a matter of record, in the past no non-Congress ruling arrangement at the Centre has sought to target top Congress leaders for early retirement through jailing.

The present ruling faction sees the Congress and the ideas it has represented over the decades as the principal obstacle to the gaining of political hegemony across mainland India that would be sustainable for some time.

Organisationally, the Congress is a weakened and a weak force now. Ordinarily, that should have given the Hindu Right latitude to leave the party alone. But clearly even a weak Congress is perceived to be a serious long-term threat. The worry for the RSS-BJP is the basic conception of India the Congress has proffered from its inception, even if it has spectacularly failed to live up to that conception and the ideals it has propagated.

Several other parties are also BJP's bugbears, and will doubtless be pursued—first the Left formations, although the Left is not a leading parliamentary presence, and the Bahujan Samaj Party, from which the RSS-BJP is desperate to wrench the dalit vote in order to assiduously construct the vision of India of it has propagated.

The likes of Nitish Kumar, Lalu Prasad Yadav, Arvind Kejriwal and Akhilesh Yadav are also more than likely to follow.

It is one thing to try and deliver on election promises, fail in the attempt, and then launch diversionary tactics to keep the country preoccupied with silly drama (and extraneous matters) in an effort to insulate the rulers from blame. For democracies, that is old hat. But the Modi dispensation is different.

It is radical from the far Right perspective. It seeks to

crush its opponents and use any ruse to do so. Governance can wait. Under this strategy, doing just enough to have something of propaganda value to say at the next election would suffice. When the key opponents are out of the way, the barest minimum of governance would suffice. At least that seems to be the thinking.

The government's marquee agenda was to drive out the Nehru-Gandhis and the Congress, and bring about a "Congress-mukt Bharat"- an India from which the political genus called the Congress has been drained out. This was its primary political aim in the overall ideological backdrop of selling the strident Hindutva version of Hinduism to Hindus, which they have flatly refused to take seriously although the RSS has been at it since 1925.

A dictatorship or a quasi-dictatorship does not like to brook any Opposition. Take China. It goes to ends of the earth to eradicate the Falun Gong, whose following gives the ruling party or the country's ruling cliques a fright. The fear is of a challenge being mounted in the future, even if this does not appear realistic at this stage.

India, of course, is not China. It has a developed civil society and a fairly embedded constitutional system. The task of Prime Minister Narendra Modi, BJP president Amit Shah, and RSS supremo Mohan Bhagwat is not likely to be easy. But that doesn't inhibit them from trying.

The BJP government has messed it up. Employment, prices and other key economic indicators are not satisfactory, and in the area of foreign policy, the country is having to suffer humiliation after humiliation. Indeed, India is being sought to be run on slogans—"love jihad", beef-eating, calling questioners anti-national and urging the country to "Stand Up", and the like. New empty slogans are being coined all the time and rung like heavy gongs.

As Modi and his cohorts ready themselves to celebrate their two years in office later this month, the newspapers are full of the dismissal of two Congress-run state governments through the misuse of state authority and by manipulating provisions of law and the Constitution. Students at Jawaharlal Nehru University, Hyderabad University, Jadavpur University, and in Lucknow and Allahabad are being called "anti-national" and "casteist". A year ago leading organisations of the voluntary sector were under attack for being "anti-national". This has become a tiresome refrain.

It is not just the Congress, the Left, the BJP's other political opponents, and the social liberals, which believe that the present government is launched on an authoritarian—even semi-dictatorial—path. Such fears are being expressed within BJP circles, where the primary apprehension being expressed is that a clique is running away with the game. Nevertheless, Modi and the BJP chief still seem to be sitting pretty. And this is because the people have not risen up.

Asian Age & The Deccan Chronicle, May 9, 2016

Neither Cricket Nor Literature

The resolution passed "unanimously" by the Sahitya Akademi (SA)—which still pretends it is India's National Academy of Letters, no less—at its special meeting on October 23, leaves little doubt that it is about as "autonomous" as the IITs, with which the minister for human resources development has been playing ducks and drakes with abandon to force top technologists and scientists out of IIT boards in order to allow saffron-hued "Vedic" technology chaps in.

Writers across the country were waiting to see the SA's bared soul at that meet before deciding what they should do with their SA awards when fellow-writers were returning their prizes in droves to protest the atmosphere of intolerance, suffocation and violence unleashed in the country by communalised Hindu crazies, who seemed to be going about their business without a care for a year or more.

The circumstances of throwing away the awards by a galaxy of writers, the *crème de la crème* of Indian literature, and a couple of creative artists (who gave back their Sangeet Natak Akademi Award), are well known and bear no retelling.

The murder of the Kannada litterateur and rationalist M.M. Kalburgi and SA's public silence over the outrage was a part of it. The murder by a lynch-mob of a Muslim villager in Uttar Pradesh's Dadri was also a part of it in the wider sense of the build-up of an atmosphere of violence against those who think or pray differently, or eat and dress differently, from the codes laid down by the proliferating saffron *sansthas* or institutions.

For the writers, relinquishing the accolade was not to do with a particular episode. It had to do with wrought emotion produced by a sense of a creative intellect's sense of helplessness and despair—a kind of loss of identity, of autonomy—over an extended period of time.

Writers can only hit back with their awards, as the poet Keki N. Daruwalla has said. In such an atmosphere, the SA president, Vishwanath Prasad Tiwari, went public with this craven remark: "If the Sahitya Akademi jumps in and protests against the restriction of the freedom of speech, then will it not divert from its primary work?"

In other words, if writers and thinkers are threatened or killed, and this causes the freedom of speech or expression to be extinguished or curtailed, then it is none of SA's business. So, presumably in Dr Tiwari's reading, the primary work of the "autonomous" body he heads is to give awards (and carry on doing so even when free speech is guillotined and writers of any mark cannot emerge).

This may be expected from a man bearing the burden of such an understanding to seek to lacerate Nayantara Sahgal with words that even a pettifogging bureaucrat may be too squeamish to muster, his sense of self-importance notwithstanding.

The SA chief, who was outraged by Sahgal's gall in giving back the prize, said things to this effect: "The Akademi made her famous. It translated her works. She has returned the award. But has she paid back the rupees one lakh that go with the citation?"

Of course Sahgal did that (even in these supersonic times it takes a cheque some time to travel), and while doing so reminded the Akademi president of the lofty aims and yardstick that had been set for the awards body in times past.

As chairman of SA (besides being Prime Minister), Nehru had chided Soviet leader Nikita Khrushchev in 1958, when Moscow (with which India had the best of relations by then), threatened Boris Pasternak with exile if the great writer—the author of Doctor Zhivago—went to Sweden to collect the Nobel Prize for literature that he had been awarded.

Nehru then proceeded to hold a press conference where he held that a writer of note must be respected even if his views differed from that of the country. Nehru's standards were usually unattainably high, and there is little hope of the likes of Dr Tiwari even approximating it.

But the SA *apparatchik* could have spared us this self-serving paean contained in the concluding part of the October 23 resolution: The SA executive committee (which he presided over) "unanimously endorses the diligent and vigilant leadership of the president to keep the dignity of the Akademi intact", etc.

The SA president- whose peers were disdaining his leadership of the Akademi by returning their award- signed the words of self-praise, unmindful that the culture of no land sanctions self-exaltation.

But what is at the core of the infamous resolution? It shamefacedly exhorts the writers to take back their returned award merely because (now), it says, it "strongly" protests the Kalburgi killing. And then there is also some galling advice—that the "Center" (yes, with this American spelling) and the states should maintain "peaceful co-existence in society", and that the various communities should "put aside the differences on grounds of caste, religion, region and ideology".

This plainly means that ordinary people of different communities are guilty of fighting one another and are creating an unbearable situation, and that the saffron ideologues and their servitors have nothing to do with the goings-on.

This is exactly what the Sangh Parivar foot soldiers trot out on television. They say one other thing most prominently—that since law and order is a state subject, the state governments (and the parties that rule them) should be hauled up for the horrible crimes that are becoming routine; in short, the proponents of Hindutva are absolved.

In this view, the Centre—the government of Prime Minister

Narendra Modi—is being unfairly targeted by writers and other artists because of ideological differences, and that the stifling atmosphere that engulfs us- the "rising intolerance" that the dissenting writers spoke of- is not a national question.

The October 23 SA document flags exactly the same issues, and in just the same way. Note especially the parsing of its argument, the reference to the "states". Going by this argument, the demolition of the Babri mosque was not a national issue but a Uttar Pradesh state issue, and that for the 2002 post-Godhra violence and spread of hatred in Gujarat the state government was cynically targeted by opponents on account of an ideological dissonance with the then chief minister.

Thank you, autonomous Sahitya Akademi, for a command performance of a high order.

Asian Age & The Deccan Chronicle, October 26, 2015

Our Nation Sanskritised

The most striking thing about militant organisations which rally people in the name of religion, and seek to achieve their ends by singling out the "other" and attacking them, is that their beliefs are completely lacking in compassion, justice or any notions taken from any humanist tradition.

Naturally, they have no kinship with the ideals of democracy, and no value for the idea of living together and sharing our common pool of resources—which is just what Pope Francis, the "poor man's pope", spoke about at the United Nations last week, and which form the core precepts of the UN—the ending of wars, promotion of peace and helping uplift the poor.

Outfits such as Lashkar-e-Tayyaba and the Islamic State of Iraq and Syria readily come to mind in this context because they revel in their notoriety. In India, the Rashtriya Swayamsevak Sangh (RSS) is not a stereotype of these threatening groups. But in its ideology—based on seeking to arouse racial and religious consciousness and directing hatred and malevolent force against people they would like to eliminate or diminish—and in its less than transparent organisational structures and functioning, India's Hindutva hotspot is moved by a similar manic energy and ambition.

The RSS' bible is 'We or Our Nationhood Defined', written by M.S. Golwalkar back in 1939, a year before he was nominated head of the organisation. It is replete with Hitlerite ideas. The RSS' offspring Bharatiya Janata Party dare not publicly endorse them. But it cannot repudiate them either.

Indeed the author is treated with reverence not only by the RSS but also other members of the Sangh Parivar and adorned with the honorific of "Pujya Guruji" ('our respected Teaches') for laying a firm ideological foundation for the faithful.

An infamous passage from his text reads: "...the foreign races in Hindustan must either adopt the Hindu culture and language, must learn to respect and hold in reverence Hindu religion, must entertain no idea but those of the glorification of the Hindu race and culture, i.e., of the Hindu nation and must lose their separate existence to merge in the Hindu race, or may stay in the country, wholly subordinate to the Hindu nation, claiming nothing, deserving no privileges, far less preferential treatment—not even citizens' rights. There is, at least should be, no other course for them to adopt."

Such chilling ideas cannot inspire votaries of equality of any stripe, leave alone the young in this country who look for equal opportunities, most urgently in the fields of education and work, in order to live peaceful lives free from want—true change and "achche din" ('good times'). It is hard to see how any of Golwalkar's postulates can make for societal harmony and progress.

But surprisingly, some policy outlines of the present regime seem to be rooted in the former RSS chief's ideas of an ideal society and state in India at the heart of which is not rational and scientific inquiry, but the privileging of so-called Hindu consciousness or outlook.

Education seems to be the most conspicuous victim under human resources development minister Smriti Irani. She has prostrated herself before the saffron outlook in order to advance her career. This can be seen from the appointment of a spurious historian as the head of the Indian Council of Historical Research, from the attempt to fill leading educational institutions with those spouting RSS' "cultural" theology which treats myth as history, and from quarters being given to Dinanath Batra, an apparatchik, in setting the schools curriculum.

The current RSS chief has also plunged straight into politics and raised questions relating to positive discrimination and affirmative action for traditionally deprived sections, though he has had to hastily cover his tracks when faced with counter-attacks from BJP's opponents in Bihar, where preparations are on for the Assembly election.

Golwalkar's signal contribution to the Hindutva belief system is his idea of "cultural nationalism", from which every odious notion in the passage cited above springs, as the former Sarsanghchalak or RSS chief himself makes clear in his work.

It also becomes plain that Prime Minister Narendra Modi's most recent attack on "secularists" in Ireland, through which he noted that his secular opponents will question any attention being paid to the Sanskrit language, is aligned to a longer trajectory.

The jibe is, of course, ill-founded. Many leading lights of Sanskrit scholarship have been sturdy secular intellectuals-some of them Marxists- who are objects of RSS' hate as much as Muslims and Christians. The economics Nobel Laureate Amartya Sen once publicly offered to engage in a discussion on Hindu scriptures and philosophy in the Sanskrit language with anyone interested. But the Hindutva brigade made themselves scarce, after having earlier taunted him.

It is doubtful there is one Sanskritist amongst them. They are, after all, politicos in disguise, not masters of Sanskrit language or literature or Hindu religious divines.

The point, however, is not the alleged aversion of secularists to Sanskrit, but the Prime Minister rooting his barb pertaining to the ancient language in the postulates of "Pujya Guruji", though he is careful to avoid saying so.

In the Golwalkar system, five "unities"—geography, race, religion, culture and language—together make the "nation", and the linguistic gap is filled for the "Hindu nation" by Sanskrit, "the dialect of the Gods", in the RSS ideologue's own words.

As much as attacking his secular opponents, Modi was

evidently airing the Golwalkar standpoint in Ireland on his way to the UN in New York where he would, with political correctness, speak of the ancient Indian concept of "Vasudhaiva Kutumbakam"—the world being one family. The real point seemed to be that one is less than a Hindu if one does not sing hymns in praise of "the dialect of the Gods".

With the BJP's own majority in Lok Sabha, although the win rested on a flimsy 31 per cent vote share, the RSS is trying to spread itself wide. The Prime Minister and his Cabinet colleagues rushing to a RSS forum to present a report card of their government is a sign that is especially repugnant to our parliamentary system.

Imagine the Prime Minister of Pakistan—although the country is hardly a democracy—loping up to the Lashkar-e-Tayyaba bosses in similar fashion, or the US President working to please the "White nationalist" Ku Klux Klan.

In Egypt, Muslim Brotherhood entered government on a sweeping vote, but botched its opportunity due to ideological over-zealousness. The RSS faithful didn't get into office on a revolutionary upsurge and have even less reason for hope.

Asain Age, September 28, 2015

Modi Right or Far Right?

The hopeful candidate of a year ago had three characteristics—he boasted, he denounced, and he made entreaties; he begged the people for their vote even as he regaled them with made-up stories about those onhigh. But the boot is now on the other leg. Prime Minister Narendra Modi is on test.

Only the credulous would have believed that there was so much black money abroad which the Modi government would bring back within 100 days and credit rupees 15,000 to the bank account of every Indian. The Modi government itself now does not believe that lie circulated at election time.

Ministers tell us that there are difficulties about the return of the black money, and in any case there is no proper way of knowing how much of it there is. But we are an understanding people. We won't hold the government accountable on the black money issue. We will treat it as election time gas.

But the jobs data, the data on prices, the corruption indices, are also not of the order that would enthuse anybody, least of all those most in need; the promised "achche din", or good times, still seem distant.

"There is a lot of sizzle, but where's the steak?" asked the stalwart journalist Arun Shourie, who was a minister in the earlier National Democratic Alliance government of Atal Behari Vajpayee. And yet, those who voted Modi in are holding faith. They have not given up on their man. They are still hoping he would deliver.

Some indication of this can be had from the recent state election results. Except the small state of Haryana, which the

BJP won hands down, elsewhere the party improved on its previous performances but failed to romp home. At the same time, no other party got in even with a chance.

The clear message is that the people are waiting for Modi to make good on his promises. They haven't lost all hope. In other words, they are not yet ready to say that they goofed up in their choice of the man.

They would keenly watch the Budget. Not just the haves, not just the industrial empires, but also those who put in a hard day's work, those waiting in the jobs queue, the middle class and others- and also the Hindu who marched with the Hindutva brigades and raised the saffron war cries. In the end they would demand nothing less than their bread-and-butter price. These are quite apart from the children of the other gods who are waiting to judge the government on fair play and equal treatment.

Modi partisans are patting themselves on their backs about the recent ordinances the government has passed, and are denouncing the Opposition for being obstreperous and quarrelsome. They argue the ordinances are the Prime Minister's way of saying he means business, that he means "development", the clever shorthand used these days for the advancement of industrial and commercial interests.

The executive orders being converted into short-term laws under the President's legislative powers certainly look to be that, but for big business chiefly. This is not anyone's idea of "development", if normal definitions are still sacrosanct. That expression denotes another paradigm—the broader theme of the uplift of all, with social sector concerns in place, and under scrutiny.

Anyhow, the top guns of industry and business are hard-nosed analysts. They know full well that ordinances will eventually have to come to parliament for endorsement. Until that happens, there will be an air of uncertainty about investments. And who is to know what will happen on the streets?

The farmers, for instance, are not likely to be amused with the ordinance declaring that their lands can now be requisitioned for industry, not many questions asked. The BJP is doing a flip-flop here. It is completely overturning the law brought by the earlier United Progressive Alliance government it had supported in 2013 when it was in the Opposition.

The Modi government now wants deregulation for industry, meaning letting it grow without hindrance, but will direct farmers even in multi-cropped areas to part with their land for industry—a kind of nationalisation, done softly, quietly. This makes for disquiet, not stability.

The forthcoming Budget, the first document under a fullfledged BJP government to detail policy perspectives within the limits imposed by public finances, will naturally raise expectations among all sections of society. The Prime Minister is certainly aware of this. At a recent gathering, he spoke of not just simplifying taxes, but also of targeted subsidies, and growth for all.

The point, however, is how well his finance minister can balance the competing claims of all sections that await a share of the pie. Just consider that none of the ordinances passed is aimed at leading the poor guy over the scaffolding. What if it had? What would the judgment of Modi's flatterers be then?

One thing is clear enough. Leaving the well-off with bulging pockets is not going to meet the aspirations of the people. It spells a risky ideological slant. The expectation that cutting taxes will automatically lead to investments, and the spread of prosperity and good cheer, is worse than naive. It can be dangerous. The schema has never worked in any country, and won't in a society riven with inequities.

Not to put too fine a point on it, "development" cannot be left in the hands of the industrial or business classes alone. Arun Jaitley is just repeating the logic the Republicans put forward in America, and typically they have left behind hurting times.

If the finance minister is serious about what he says, there could be trouble ahead. A sense of ease in the country is not limited to the ease of doing business. That is something the leaders of the government can choose to overlook at their own peril, and to the country's cost.

Modi is heard soothing industrial interests and foreign businesses often enough. Doors are wide open for them. But who has heard him quell doubts about social peace, routinely being sought to be endangered by communal fanatics? We need to know—is Modi just Right, or Far Right?

Asian Age & The Deccan Chronicle, January 19, 2015

Nationalism, Not Hindu Nationalism

Even as the Lok Sabha results were streaming in, many were rolling up their sleeve in glee—their hour had come; they were getting ready to dismantle, and then bury fathoms deep, what after Jawaharlal Nehru's death has come to be known as the "Nehruvian consensus".

Try as they might—and there will be no lack of effort there, both in the government and outside of it—the Nehru-sceptics are likely to soon realise that the edifice of Nehruvian constructs does not rest on quick sand, that it is rooted in our history as well as our current reality, and therefore won't be easy to get rid of.

Even a government led by the most ardent Rashtriya Swayamsevak Sangh *pracharak* or whole-time propagandist, who would love to double-wrestle Nehru and his ideas all the way to the farthest *akhara* or wrestling pit, is likely to find it near impossible to consign the first Prime Minister's basic thinking about India's history and society to the dung heap.

Narendra Modi, now that he is our Prime Minister, or others speaking in the name of his government, may proceed to do all manner of undesirable things that may comfort the RSS—such as infiltrate the administrative and security apparatus, or seek to undermine the validity of scientific education and evaluations and promote hocus-pocus (for instance, the academically ridiculed notion that India was always the home of the Aryans who, on account of their prowess, spread to other parts of the world from here) in the name of upholding Indian (this is a surreptitious short-hand for "Hindu alone") culture and values.

But such enthusiasts of the Hindu Far Right, abetted without shame by the high priests of the market-alone principle in public affairs, are likely to be defeated before their own eyes. Nehru believed, for instance, (and he drew this also from Mahatma Gandhi, from whom, in particular, his social beliefs gained great strength) that this ancient land belongs to all those who live here even if they came only a few hundred years ago, unlike the Aryan invading hordes who arrived a few thousand years ago.

It follows that no group or community can take precedence over any other in the name of religion, ethnicity, or caste and tribe, for that would be another name for discrimination. This was not merely a matter of adhering to the grand juridical principle of equality before the law, but also suffusing that idea with social sanction and acceptance in our hearts.

Thus, by virtue of being a part of the majority Hindu religious community, a *dhoti* and *teeka*-wearing Hindu traditionalist cannot claim superior rights in society (leave alone the law) over a burqa-wearing Muslim woman or a Christian prominently displaying the sign of the cross.

To their credit, many influential Hindu traditionalists—in the past as well as now—have sturdily upheld equal rights for non-Hindus. Gandhi and Swami Vivekananda are strong examples of this. For that matter, so was Sardar Vallabhbhai Patel, whose idea of India—as evident in his policy actions as home minister—did not include privileging the Hindus over other religious communities.

This is seen, above all, in his integration of all princely states, Hindu and Muslim alike, with equal vigour in a certain framework of a democratic, newly-emergent, post-colonial India. (If Modi and the RSS school seek to give the impression of being Patelites, rather than Gandhian or Nehruvian, it is because they wish to link themselves through Patel to the freedom movement in which they did not participate as a group, and because Patel had several policy differences with

Nehru, whom they abhor).

These epochal men were "nationalist", not "Hindu nationalist", unlike our present Prime Minister, who embraced the latter tag with frightening enthusiasm in the recent election campaign without a whimper of protest from the liberal camp who forgot even their basics merely because they wanted to fight the Congress. How would the liberals have reacted, one wonders, if a prominent Muslim politician got up and called himself an "Islamic nationalist"?

Unlike the RSS and its cohorts, Gandhi and Vivekananda wanted to despatch British (they did not call it Christian) colonialism and create a sovereign and equal India. They had no mind to restore a Hindu India of the pre-medieval type, which is what the votaries of Hindutva were after.

It is the ethos of the Hindu nationalist that the RSS and its kindred bodies would like to see prevail in India today, although, when expedient, they swear by the Indian Constitution in which there is no place for any form of sectarian nationalism. Time will help us judge whether Prime Minister Modi furthers the cause of Hindu nationalism, or of Indian nationalism.

Nehru was also a strong votary of two other powerful notions—his idea of "socialism" and of "nonalignment". In a desperately poor country—in which extensive pockets of intense poverty conspicuously remain—he was persuaded that a government-led direct assault on poverty (and its social consequences) was an inescapable necessity.

This did not mean condoning the siphoning off of government funds meant for anti-poverty programmes, as well as bank deposits, by powerful vested interests (including capitalist fat-cats). If through "good governance" which he promises, Modi can eliminate or vastly reduce the scope for such corruption, India will be a more wholesome, a more equal, and a happier place.

Will his government move in this direction, besides promoting investments? Or, will it cut programmes for positive discrimination in favour of the poor, citing that as the only way to achieve financial stability? A good deal of the politics outside parliament may depend on that and impact parliament itself even if the government has unassailable numbers at present.

Nehru's "nonalignment" has been ideologically assaulted by quarters that desire India to surrender its autonomy of action on the international stage to Western—chiefly US—conceptions of the world order. Essentially, this is an assault on the idea of a democratic India that is "strong" and determines its own moorings.

The Bharatiya Janata Party government will naturally be watched on all fronts, especially that of Hindu nationalism versus Indian nationalism, which is the crucible of a Nehruvian, even a Gandhian consensus.

Asian Age & The Deccan Chronicle, January 9, 2015

The Republic of RSS

This may be Narendra Modi's government, but India may be on its way to becoming Rashtriya Swayamsevak Sangh's republic. The signs point that way. The government is either helpless, or is a silent accomplice—silent because it still wishes to be seen as upholding the panoply of democracy.

Not doing so could be risky at this stage when the RSS, its progenitor, still enjoys only limited influence in the country, and is by no means ready for a takeover (although its *firmans* ring loud and menacing). That day could come if things go badly for India, strategically speaking. We are far from there, though.

One reason is we are way too big for the RSS, or any totalitarian thought—and also way too diverse, especially in the mainland of Hindu terrain that the RSS has been trying for 90 years to homogenise.

"RSS republic" is a signifier since the Hindutva mother-body seeks to glamorise itself as the torchbearer of Hindu society and falsely presents itself as the renewer of Hinduism, its *mojadidi*. Witness its shrill and deeply divisive " ghar wapsi " or re-conversion pitch aimed at converting, foremost, the petty bourgeois and poor class Hindu (its presumed votebank) to its cause.

The supporting noise from senior Bharatiya Janata Party leaders in positions of power is revealing. It points to close coordination with an unelected outfit—which is transformed into an extra-constitutional authority when the BJP assumes power with a majority of its own in Parliament.

Prime Minister Narendra Modi has tactically avoided lending his voice to the re-conversion cacophony. Hence his deafening silence in Parliament. He has perforce to be mindful of his constitutional status when his cohorts are running a campaign that is repugnant to the Constitution.

The notion of a "republic" associated with any religion is dubious, for a republic is, by definition, founded on non-sectarian principles that embrace the equality of citizens, irrespective of faith or hierarchies. But the idea of a Hindu republic is doubly confounding.

Unlike the so-called Islamic republics, which are governed by the basic laws of Islam (and are less of a republic), there can be no basic laws of Hinduism governing a Hindu republic. These simply don't exist. A Hindu view of state has not been propounded. The RSS is not about to propound one. It simply can't. In fact, it is not a body of Hindus in any religious sense. It is a deep-going political outfit. It is also no doubt a serious player.

The RSS seeks to ride to power and retain it for the long term by continuing to mobilise citizens in the name of the religion of the majority and presenting the minorities as the hostile "other". Witness, for instance, the "Ramzada-haramzada" (children of the Hindu deity Lord Rama versus bastard children, a vulgar way of referring to Indian Muslims, given the context) dichotomy emphasised by a Union minister.

Confrontations with the past are set up; the imagined victims of history sought to be consoled as part of the ploy. But since this alone won't do in the democratic jostle at elections, the saffron leadership plays on secular slogans and the past mistakes of non-sectarian political parties.

Its *mantra* at present is "development", although in the six months in which its representatives have adorned top office, there are few steps taken in that direction, if "development" is understood to be the use of national resources for the betterment of the lives of the people, particularly those most in need. In fact, the opposite has been observed.

A fat cat like Adani, a known bag carrier of Modi since his days as chief minister, has been given a loan of one billion US dollars or about rupees 6,000 crore by the SBI to invest in Australia. Did he first try the private banks—in India or Australia? Has any other industrialist received such a fat purse from any public bank in a single transaction? More, was due diligence done by SBI in advancing the loan?

Probably not, since the magnitudes are awe-inspiring. So, did the government weigh in at the highest level? Probably yes. This is as clear-cut a definition of crony capitalism as one might expect. Therefore, just to clarify matters, should there be an investigation by appropriate authorities under Supreme Court guidance? Indubitably yes. We can't have such staggering sums vanishing into one man's pocket and wait for non-performing assets (NPAs, or loans not returned) to pile up.

If this is what the trope of "development" and "good governance" can be reduced to under the tallest men of the BJP guided by the RSS, then God help us.

By the same token of good governance, this year Gandhi Jayanti (October 2) was shoved into the background by the PM's "Swachh Bharat Abhiyan" (the cleaning up of streets by preening politicians) calculatedly inaugurated on the same day; Indira Gandhi's death anniversary on October 31 was sent to the dustbin in favour of Sardar Vallabhbhai Patel's birth anniversary the same day; the Christmas day nearly sent packing (but for a media outcry) in favour of holding an essay-writing and declamation contest in schools; and the old Planning Commission disbanded though another body or bodies will be doing similar things. That is RSS', and by association the BJP's, distillation of the idea of development and good governance.

But what's their view of parliamentary democracy that our Constitution decrees? How do they propose to manage state power in a democratic way to further the institutions of democracy? Or, is the game really to concentrate power in the hands of a leader who will advance the agenda of the RSS, a quasi-secret body? We need look no farther than at the conduct of government by Modi and his relationship to Parliament.

Modi clearly looks down upon parliament. He hardly ever sets foot in its chambers to engage on policy issues with the Opposition. He shuns discussions on matters agitating the public sphere even in his public appearances. Two-way interactions with the media—where questions are asked—are history. Modi's ministers have been frightened into submission. The bureaucracy reports to work on time, but is kept busy looking over its shoulder.

We have arrived at the most graphic case of the leader at the top as the issuer of instruction and the great thriver on state propaganda—the 'one leader syndrome' at its most succinct.

Asian Age & The Deccan Chronicle, December 22, 2014

The Quiet Republic

There are times when analysis is not needed; silence says it all. The air is still, as on a moisture-laden day. There is little expectation of rain, for it hasn't rained even when the clouds have dutifully lined up. Yes, it is the suffocating stillness after the noisy Lok Sabha election—in which Narendra Modi did all the talking, so much talking—which is the worry. Modi is now silent.

He also seems to have made himself unapproachable. Let alone the media, the Prime Minister's top colleagues hint they can see him only if he wants to see them, meaning if he summons them.

Meanwhile, whether they have received an instruction, or are just not taking chances with the boss, they too have gone silent.

Ruling party MPs—even ministers—hurry past the Central Hall, the space between the two chambers of Parliament which has served as the leisurely gathering ground over endless cups of tea or coffee of politicians and senior journalists over the decades, where speech is unhindered, unhampered, and off the record, and where MPs who joust with one another inside the House can cosy up as chums.

When they were in the Opposition, the Bharatiya Janata Party leaders would expostulate, pontificate, hold court, and unburden themselves of schemes and political plots, even if these were only inside their heads. Today, however, they say their worst fears will come true if they are spotted by Mr Modi's look-out boys speaking with politicians of rival parties or, worse still, journalists.

Perhaps the real fear is that the BJP MPs might spend too much time confabulating with one another, for that has the makings of something more complex than just the fixing of a little deal.

The PM's spotters have been found in Central Hall on a regular basis of late. They are minor bureaucrats but have caused not a little dread in the BJP ranks in parliament. Who wants to be reported for hobnobbing with the press, derided by Modi as "news merchants" during the long election campaign?

Nobody wants Big Brother to watch, and so it is deemed best to make sure there is nothing there to watch. It's not just the BJP's abandoned mentor and old warhorse Lal Krishna Advani who has retreated into a shell. The whole party has gone quiet. It is as though it has ceased to exist so soon after an election victory of historic proportions.

Daily briefings for the press, routine for decades, have suddenly stopped. The Prime Minister's Office too has no spokesman. If a journalist wishes to meet a senior PMO official, there are no channels through which this can be made to happen.

The day of handout journalism has arrived, typical of authoritarian regimes—so reminiscent of the days of the Emergency that the BJP leaders denounce to their heart's content even 40 years after the event in a bid to squeeze out political mileage from a lemon that has long rotted. Newspapers thus publish what is officially given out, for nothing else is possible as there is a virtual gag order. Official propaganda is making a comeback.

After the BJP trounced its opponents in the election under Modi's leadership, now the unquestioned leader bowed low and deep to touch with his forehead the stone on the steps of Parliament House which he was entering for the first time in his life.

It was an extraordinary spectacle and the country watched

admiringly. India's first PM from Hindutva ranks was to take oath of office with a majority of his own, unlike Atal Behari Vajpayee who had been hemmed in by grasping coalition partners.

Naturally much was expected from such a man, first of all the refurbishing of democratic governance. A leading MP of a regional party from Orissa spoke breathlessly (and in the view of some of his colleagues, foolishly and prematurely) in a television programme the other day of the PM's passionate commitment to democracy, for this is what the gesture on the steps signified to him.

Alas, the inner contours of the government remain unseen as they have been obscured from view with apparent deliberation. The PM hardly ever attends parliament. (We can't any more go to town questioning Rahul Gandhi's record of low attendance in parliament.) This is a sharp deviation from tradition.

Modi's many distinguished predecessors would either be personally present in the House, or if busy on government work made sure they were frequently updated on Parliament proceedings in the course of a day. It was a rare exception if any of them went abroad for a multilateral conference or a bilateral summit when parliament was in session.

The PM deferred to parliament—yes, even the all-powerful Indira Gandhi could occasionally be seen walking with rapid strides to get to the House if an important Opposition leader was slated to speak. The mood of the Opposition in Parliament conveyed to successive PMs the temper of the country. How things have changed!

The present Indian leader is made of different stuff. Since he doesn't attend parliament much, at the Tuesday meetings of the BJP Parliamentary Party, he is said to gesture the BJP leaders of both Houses to summarise for him the week's goings-on. He has perfected the art of controlling his MPs and ministers.

By ensuring the election of his acolyte Amit Shah, who still has much answering to do before law courts for many alleged past misdemeanours, as president of BJP, Modi's control over the organisational machinery of the ruling party is also now absolute. As a journalist said only half in jest, the PM will now seek to ensure that it is he who gets to decide who the next Rashtriya Swayamsevak Sangh chief will be.

Is the stillness that surrounds us the stillness that attends on sterility? Are we looking at sterile times ahead, whose backlash can presage chaos? Or, does the strangeness of the air signify a more disagreeable eeriness? We shall, of course, soon find out as the story unfolds.

Only two-thirds of the hands-off one hundred days—the so-called "honeymoon period" of a newly elected government—are done. The media will stick to schedule and won't step out of line before that. After that, let's hope it won't continue to remain a mute Modi-loyalist.

Asian Age & The Deccan Chronicle, August 4, 2014

Decorum in Political Theatre

Frequent remarks of senior Bharatiya Janata Party leader and Madhya Pradesh Chief Minister Shivraj Singh Chouhan, while projecting his achievements, or answering critics of his party and government even in the election season, are a reminder of a certain decorum in public discourse that is all too frequently eclipsed these days by party leaders on all sides who are persuaded that being brash, clever, snide, half-truthful and loud is what makes them forceful, important and appealing.

Chouhan's approach stands out for its moderation, sense of balance, and the upholding of a certain dignity that is associated with the conduct of senior and serious public figures in all democracies, especially in India where extending courtesies even to opponents still earns approbation—yes, even by the young generation—and is part of a long tradition of public discourse.

Many associate the decline in civility with the rise of subaltern politics and the emergence of leaders who did not spring from privileged caste or class backgrounds. The case of Chouhan—or for that matter Bihar chief minister Nitish Kumar—is a direct refutation of such an elitist view in which goodness, uprightness and ability are linked with the highborn.

Gujarat leader Narendra Modi, who has been handpicked by the Rashtra Swayamsevak Sangh to lead the BJP to power, alas is not the epitome of public values or virtues that appear to mark the public persona of Mr Chouhan. As Modi strides the land with his dramatic flourishes, crowd-pulling play of words that rhyme but seem bereft of reason, it is hard to say if he strikes a chord in his listeners who are not already converted to his world and his worldview.

Chouhan, on the other hand, has an impact if one is attentive. Apparently the RSS—and finally, the BJP—have plumped for Modi for the theatre he provides in our image-driven times. He dresses up for the show, changing his attire, choosing his colours, being finicky, being trendy. This may be the outcome of the labours of the US public relations firm he hired to help him change his brand from the dour RSS "karyakarta" or volunteer chief minister who would brook no dissent, who presided over times when a months-long pogrom proceeded unhindered in Gujarat, to a new avatar of seeming modernity, contemporaneity, even inclusiveness—a man of action, the one who can pull your chestnuts out of the fire.

Some of this does certainly wash as people come across a new kind of political personality who is keen to cut a dash, who measures his stride in particular ways for effect, who nurtures a walk that is in your face. Thus, when he strikes a stance on stage and menacingly intones "shehzade" ("prince"- to mock Rahul Gandhi), some are reminded instinctively of the Emperor Akbar in the film Mughal-e-Azam addressing Prince Salim with authority that comes naturally to the master of all men.

Those who are struck by the parallel, however, do also observe that it is the prince who eventually has his way. Trying to imprint your personality on others without commanding the weight of substance can have its pitfalls, though. Modi's first major public event in Delhi was his speech this year to the students of Shri Ram College of Commerce, an institution known to produce high-value business executives and nurture entrepreneurial talent and drive.

This was exactly right for a political leader who has given industrialists everything they need on concessional terms and with surprising speed. Hordes of students came to listen and dutifully told television cameras how impressed they were. The show was a national media event as news analysis and editorials followed on the trail of gushing news reports.

It was assumed by most that the young, aspirational, India had found its talisman in Modi—that they were tired of old-style politics, impatient with bureaucracy with its elliptical ways and systemic rigidity and aridness, that they wanted instant change even if this was not accompanied with reflection. But a surprising event was to follow.

When college elections were held at SRCC (Arun Jaitley's college), BJP lost every key post and the Congress took everything. Oddly enough, this was at a time when in the election for the Delhi University Students' Union, the BJP students' wing had claimed nearly every top position. Now, the BJP is not a party without support in Delhi and in Delhi's colleges. So, what appeared to have transpired was that the metropolitan elite boys and girls of a decidedly elite college had seen through the magic-maker. After all, they are not without the power of analysis.

None of this was reported in the Delhi papers. However, a small news item did appear in far away Mumbai. In his SRCC speech, Modi spoke of "India First". He does that in every speech now. The unspoken assumption is that for the rest of us India is dispensable. The one inkling the Gujarat leader gave of his policy orientation was when he said he believed that the smaller the government, the happier the populace. This seems straight out of the catechism of America's Republican Party.

As Modi has gone about his quest for national power, he seems to have been careful not to repeat the far-right economic ideology. May be he has been told by his party to tone it down. After all, the poor too live here and you can't woo them unless the government shows itself ready to intervene on their behalf.

To make up for the paucity of policy imagination, the PM aspirant has taken to demagogy with passion. He invokes "Italy", "Rome", "dynasty" as he rails against the Congress. This does raise an occasional titter, but it is a beaten theme, or the result of the last two elections might have been different. It would be far more refreshing to see a new aspirant for power come forward with bold ideas on industry, agriculture, poverty removal, dealing with difficult neighbours, and the like. But it's been a clean slate so far.

Asian Age & The Deccan Chronicle, October 28, 2013

KASHMIR

Kashmir's Congested Political Space is Costing Its Younger Generation

There is acute political awareness in Kashmir, and the nuances of the game are understood even among its younger residents. In that respect, the Valley may be thought of as being among the most politically alive regions of the country.

There is no shortage of political parties on the ground. There is also the separatist combine—the Hurriyat Conference. In a freer atmosphere, Kashmir may have buzzed with political activity.

Enough has happened in state in the past year to have ensured this—the toppling of the Mehbooba Mufti-led government, the imposition of Governor's rule, the Valley-wide raising of temperatures on the ill-concealed effort of the BJP to do away with Article 35-A of the constitution through hostile judicial action as well as the virtually fraudulent municipal bodies' election.

Governor Satya Pal Malik's failure to permit a coalition of the PDP-NC-Congress to form an alternative government on the specious ground that such an arrangement might make the security forces "insecure" has caused disquiet among the people.

And the Modi regime's adamant refusal over the years to hold talks with the political elements in the Valley in order to ease the atmosphere has been a persistent cause of sullenness and despair. In short, political pathways appear to have been deliberately jammed.

In contrast, the present writer can recall unbelievable

scenes of mass participation in the poll campaigns of political parties in the run-up to the assembly election of 2002, when the atmosphere became freer after the collapse of the 1990s insurgency. Towns and even the bigger villages had suddenly come alive with peaceful politics, although Pakistan-backed terrorist shootings and bombings still dominated headlines.

Today, sadly, what compels a visitor's attention is the choking of channels of political articulation. Persistent violence has been the most conspicuous outcome. This has been most evident in the southern districts of Kashmir. In fact, today this remains the only brand of overt 'politics' on view.

The principal actors in this drama are teenagers and young men. Engaging the security forces on a recurrent basis is their platform of action. And every round of killings that takes place triggers further emotional upheaval in impressionable young people.

Feeling helpless and angry, they run away from home to join terror groups like the Hizbul Mujahideen and local units of Pakistan-based outfits such as the Lashkar-e-Tayyaba. They receive weapons and a few days of light training. Within weeks, these young men are dead in foolish encounters with the security forces. Another cycle of quitting home to become martyrs ensues.

This is senseless. A new generation is being lost. But when channels of normal politics are clogged on account of New Delhi's Kashmir policy of the past four years to let only the gun do the talking, a messy result that turns lives upside down is perhaps inevitable.

This, however, is only a part of the story. A visible disturbing trend is the flaring of pro-Pakistan sentiment among the impressionable youth. Careful non-official observers of the scene attest to this. There is all round a sense of tragedy foretold. President's rule, imposed on December 20, can't alleviate the situation.

On a recent visit to the Valley, a free-wheeling conversation with the separatist leader Mirwaiz Umar Farooq, Kashmir's chief cleric, deepens the sense of despair.

Last month, around 40 freshly-minted local militants were killed in south Kashmir. A 19-month-old girl was hit in one eye by a pellet fired by the security forces. This month, seven civilians were killed when the army fired upon stone pelters.

The situation is worse than grim. The boys who are dying have turned autonomous actors, the Mirwaiz says, outside the influence of even the Hurriyat leadership. He thinks the only way out of the impasse is to de-congest the political space.

To stay relevant, the Hurriyat leadership sometimes calls for strike actions. The people grudgingly accept this if only to show solidarity with the dead. Exceptions apart, the mainstream parties no longer bother asking their followers to protest even symbolically. Normal politics has truly gone to sleep in Kashmir. This can only deepen anxieties.

The only politicians active have been the Ram Madhavs of the world, peddling RSS's wares that no Kashmiri bothers with, as the governor plies the Centre's trade.

The Wire, December 20, 2018

Satya Pal Malik Is Busy Serving the BJP's Short-Sighted Interests in J&K

Satya Pal Malik is a widely travelled man, and he knows a thing or two about defections. There probably isn't a worthwhile political entity in parliament of which he has not been, at least briefly, a part—and what a success this nondescript politician's career has been as a result.

He's a governor on the trot—first in Bihar, then the crème de la crème, Kashmir—and after the coup in Srinagar this week, he is destined to go much farther, if the BJP-RSS stays in the driver's seat.

There was no shortage of competent men, retired but fit and wise, from the services who could have been a replacement for outgoing governor N.N. Vohra, with whom Delhi was mighty displeased as he tried to be correct for the most part. The regime professes to love everything military, but it opted for a feckless, faceless, former politico. No prizes for guessing why.

In comments to the media after his appointment, Malik made a song and dance about being a politician—suggesting that he had been mandated to be a bridge between the people of Kashmir and the government in a way that a retired official couldn't be—and saying that his doors would be open day or night. But he fell at the first hurdle.

Democracy has been at a severe discount in Kashmir since long before the BJP-RSS got into the saddle. But Muslim politicians of the Valley were never before reviled and communally taunted, as is being done—directly or indirectly—in the present BJP raj.

By deepening alienation through a language of discrimination, the governor's actions and utterances have done more for the ISI's Kashmir project than the hordes of hostile armed infiltrators can ever hope to do.

In 1996, Prime Minister Narasimha Rao, at the end of the first organised insurgency, and before the first post-insurgency assembly polls, had called on the reluctant National Conference leader Farooq Abdullah to take part.

On the question of autonomy for Kashmir, the prime minister said "the sky is the limit", in his famous Ougadougou declaration from Burkina Faso. Abdullah eventually obliged and the NC formed government. The NC leader wasn't hectored or degraded by the Centre for showing initial hesitation.

The next election in 2002 threw up a fractured mandate, as the NC lost power. The Congress and the PDP took too long to come to their internal arrangement about who would lead the government first, but governor Girish Saxena, a former chief of R&AW (the country's external intelligence agency), waited patiently for the political puzzle to be solved. With him at the helm, governor's rule lasted a mere 15 days, imposed to satisfy constitutional requirements.

Saxena understood the political and emotional need of the Valley in a most difficult moment, and didn't play divisive games or disregard the Muslim leaders of J&K.

Subsequently, a BJP prime minister, Atal Behari Vajpayee, declared he would look at the Kashmir issue through the prism of "*insaniyat*", or human values. He even opened talks with a faction of Hizbul Mujahideen—which had to be abandoned on account of the principal interlocutor being murdered—as a prelude to opening talks with Pakistan.

The Modi regime has taken no lessons from the political temperament exhibited in the past by the Centre toward Kashmir. During its cohabitation of three years with the valley-based PDP, it brought governance to a standstill, before humiliating its ally. In the process, it was unable to do any favours to its own constituency in Jammu, which will be entitled to ask Modi a few searching questions.

The present governor's only achievement has been to serve the short-sighted interests of the BJP, rather than of the constitution, even as the BJP articulated its interest as being antagonistic to that of the people of Kashmir.

But the equation is simple: a government that treats all the people of the Kashmir Valley as adversaries to be subdued will come to grief and will bring India to grief. In fact, to use a much-favoured word these days, such an attitude is plain "anti-national".

Another *sutra* forgotten by the Modis, the Ram Madhavs and the Maliks of the world is that if the people of Kashmir are not on your side, you cannot negotiate anything worthwhile with Pakistan, no matter how muscular the rhetoric.

The Wire, November 24, 2018

The 'Unholy' Alliance May Be Over, But There Are Still Dark Days Ahead for Kashmir

There is no golden dawn at the end of the inglorious People's Democratic Party-Bharatiya Janata Party interregnum in Kashmir, but at least the long night is over.

Uncertainty and foreboding mark the foreseeable future. This is because the BJP still rules at the Centre, and under governor's rule it will be calling the shots with renewed communalist and militarist fervour, if that is the trajectory it reckons will suit its interests.

In determining that, its consideration will not be limited to Jammu and Kashmir, or more particularly the state's Hindu-majority Jammu division. After all, there are only two Lok Sabha seats in Jammu.

The saffronites are more likely to be concerned with the rest of the country as we slip into an election year and the BJP finds it expedient to project a macho, false, so-called "India First" image even after it has opened up the Kashmir Valley to a fresh and long bout of terrorist depredation by Pakistani jihadists and their cohorts in the Valley.

With Mehbooba Mufti's virtual sack and the perfectly planned introduction of direct rule from the Prime Minister's Office, with national security advisor Ajit Doval playing Modi's jack, the saffron party will not now have to contend with the paradoxical situation of an acquiescing state-level partner in the PDP that also raised uncomfortable questions from time to time.

This means the BJP may now run the show any way it likes and allow its "muscular" but mindless, and dangerous and morally hollow, policies unhindered play at the expense of the peace-craving population of Kashmir.

In the worst case scenario, these policies may begin to resemble what Israel is doing to the Palestinians, as there are scarily close similarities between Benjamin Netanyahu and Narendra Modi. Such policies will suffocate the Kashmir Valley, cause India immeasurable harm and earn this country regional and international odium.

There is fortuitously a reasonable chance the damage can be limited to a year as Modi's prospects for the next parliament elections seem far less assured than what his cronies pray for. At least that seems the emerging sense in the country. That is the saving grace.

In a fundamental way, the Modi rule in Kashmir has been different from what went before, and that's been the basic cause of the mess things are in. It is in this period that the "Hindu" factor was injected with cold calculation for the first time.

New Delhi overlooked the fact that India was a democracy. It trampled underfoot the well-acknowledged understanding that Indian culture was a multi-faceted wonder that was not overrun by a particular factor—religious or linguistic. It also ignored the inherent syncretism that pervades all aspects of life in Kashmir, including the religious, which the jihadists are seeking to overturn.

With RSS-BJP's ingrained communal reading of history, society and politics, New Delhi made "Hindu India" confront "Muslim Kashmir". The first disturbing sign of this came in 2015, not long after BJP got into government in J&K for the first time.

When trouble broke out between groups of students at a technology institute in Srinagar over a trivial matter, the Centre removed the J&K Police, which was doing a fine job tackling the situation, and inserted the CRPF. The CRPF also did a professional job. But the triumphalist statements of the Sangh *parivar* elements of the time let down the central force by darkly expressing satisfaction that a Hindu force would teach the Muslims a lesson.

A year on, then defence minister Manohar Parrikar turned out in RSS uniform while on a visit to Jammu, mocking the spirit of democratic India. Parrikar's devotion to political Hinduism was widely noted in the Kashmir Valley. It would, of course, have been far worse if Modi had done the same. The repercussions would have been felt far and wide. But Parrikar's touching fidelity to his real cause did not leave the Kashmiri unscathed.

Now that he is no more, his name can be revealed as there is nothing shaming in the context. The late Shujaat Bukhari, the Srinagar-based editor who sought moderate ground, preached dialogue and engagement, and was mowed down for his pains in a targeted assassination in Srinagar just before Id-ul-Fitr, had made it a point to note the deliberately provocative act of the defence minister in a contemplative, off-the-record conversation with a group of journalists from Delhi visiting Srinagar in November 2016. The findings that emerged provided the core of a published report afterward.

In the same meeting, another senior editor narrated an incident which goes to the heart of the matter. He said he once spotted a 70-year-old man in a crowd of stone-pelting youth. Utterly surprised, he asked the elderly protester why he was in a throng of hot-headed youngsters, and was humbled by the response. The old man just said, "Politics and police and military action are one thing, but I don't want a *teeka* (a Hindu-signifying vermilion mark) forcibly planted on my forehead."

The Modi regime has scrupulously avoided the politics of engagement in Kashmir, but it has without inhibition played politics of another kind—a politics to be the vehicle for its ideology which it thinks will brighten his party's electoral prospects as well.

The old man pelting stones is evidently wrong in a literal sense, for even Modi, who has skidded from one failed policy to another in his four years, wouldn't dream of the reckless enterprise of embarking on a mission of religious conversion in Kashmir. That would be too risky. His calculations are less ambitious—to persuade 'Hindu' India that he is being tough, real tough, in dealing with Muslims, and bad, real bad.

The project to impress communal Hindus in order to win them over electorally began long before the rug was pulled under the feet of Mehbooba.

The Wire, June 23, 2018

Don't Invite Chaos, or Worse, to Valley by Removing Article 35A

The Supreme Court, which on the plea of the government has deferred by two months the consideration of the RSS-inspired challenged to Article 35-A of the Constitution dealing with the sensitive issue of who may be permitted to own immoveable property in Jammu and Kashmir, would do well to be mindful that the fierce bid to have the provision scrapped is linked to political and ideological motivations of those in power, and not to constitutional, legal or economic considerations, though at the formal level it is these that are cited.

But some history needs recalling here. In real terms, 35-A is a sub-set of Article 370 of the Constitution under which Maharaja Hari Singh, the J&K ruler at the time of Independence and the Partition of India, acceded to India. It should be noted that he did not "merge" his domain into India, but "acceded" under specific conditions.

The Maharaja, although closely aligned to the RSS and its cohorts in the Jammu region, had no mind to join 'Hindu' India after Independence and had wanted to remain independent. When Pakistani irregulars nearly seized his summer capital Srinagar, he pleaded with New Delhi to save him. But he struck a bargain. The conditions are enshrined in Article 370, which is the critical bridge that links Kashmir to India.

Essentially, the Maharaja wanted to ensure continued protection- after accession to India- for the properties of his Hindu subjects, primarily the Jammu Dogras and the Kashmiri Pandits, for Kashmir valley Muslims were practically serfs then and hardly owned any land.

In 1927, responding to moves by the Dogra Pratinidhi Sabha and the Kashmiri Pandit Pratinidhi Sabha, Hari Singh had passed the State Subject Laws, whose purport was to prevent affluent elements and top civil servants from outside, principally Punjab next-door, from acquiring properties in J&K. Subsequently, under Sheikh Abdullah's Naya Kashmir programme, which brought about land ceilings, the valley Muslims too came into property and became beneficiaries of the 1927 law.

It is this law that receives protection through 35-A brought into the statutes in 1954. But 35-A does something else of no small significance. It confers Indian citizenship on J&K's "state subjects" (now known as Permanent Residents, with a few categories added). If 35-A goes, the people of Jammu, Kashmir and Ladakh will cease to be citizens of India.

In that event, Pakistan can move in with ease by throwing bridges at the Muslim communal elements in the valley, or even muscling its way in. It won't take more than a few hours for the incorporation of Kashmir valley and the Jammu region areas surrounding it into Pakistan.

Those asking for the scrapping of 35-A may then be invited to repent at leisure. The valley's independence-seekers will stand no chance at all when the Pakistani hordes come marching in, as they nearly did in October 1947.

The RSS and its offshoot the BJP are short-sighted. Essentially, their vision is to see that Hindus must dominate all aspects of life, including demographics, everywhere. To that extent, the notion of citizenship in a democracy is also to be held in abeyance, though this is never put down in black and white. In the case of J&K, the demographics can be controlled only when non-Muslims from outside J&K are permitted to buy land and property, especially in the valley, on a massive scale.

It is broadly in line with this view that the saffron brigades press for property rights and the accrual of other benefits that follow to the progeny of non-J&K refugees from the Pakistan side after Partition.

It is the denominational view of life and politics, rather than genuine republican concerns, that the apex court is being called upon to adjudicate in the guise of the petition of the RSS-linked NGO We The People, which also finds Article 370 repugnant and seeks its abrogation.

Since the removal of 370- duly brought in through the Constituent Assembly- on which there is a nationwide consensus barring RSS-BJP- will be hard for the BJP to do even when it has a comfortable majority of its own in Parliament, 35-A is being made to serve as the thin end of the wedge.

We as Indians will be inviting chaos and worse if the Supreme Court even finds the writ petitions challenging 35-A maintainable.

Economic Times, October 31, 2017

The Return of the Djinn to Kashmir

The djinn has returned to Kashmir Valley after a quarter-century—the guns are out, the blaze has started. But in New Delhi the discussion is not about how to wean the young in Kashmir away from the suicidal course of dancing to Pakistan's martial tune at the expense of their own religious traditions and culture, or on communicating with people or taking on dissenters with words that persuade, not with guns. The new formula seems to be *"boli se naheen, goli sey"*—forget talks, our guns will lead us to glory; we have the resolve.

That's why it may prove costly for Chief Minister Mehbooba Mufti- whose credibility has been destroyed by her partner, the BJP, by making her appear its vassal- to show the gumption to suggest that delaying political engagement in the Valley is conter-productive.

"Not now" is the impatient message RSS' and BJP's pointman for Kashmir, Ram Madhav, leaves behind in Srinagar on the issue of holding talks. He is silent on when, or in what conditions. Perhaps the BJP-RSS envisage that a solution can only be found when the protesting Kashmiri wears himself out.

In the Valley, they are calling this the "Doval doctrine", after national security adviser Ajit Doval. They are wrong. A doctrine of such sweep, which places India's democracy and national integration on the line, must be owned by Prime Minister Narendra Modi himself. The NSA is just a bureaucrat.

Instead of embedding India's security in integrative democratic politics, the discussion instigated by the BJP is on raising the propaganda pitch of Hindutva through "nationalism".

Phoney nationalistic fervour is being force-fed at cinemas where the national anthem is played at the start of every show. At universities, there is a race to please the HRD ministry. Vice-chancellors scurry to find the tallest pole on which to hoist the national standard—in the making of which the *kisan-mazdoor* (the peasant and the worker) played the stellar role while Hindutvawadis played no part at all—so that the young may be encouraged to "breathe the spirit of nationalism".

Meanwhile, Kashmir conspicuously slips into strategic anarchy and violence which, going by the signs, can only presage tragedy. School and college girls are now filing out and hurling stones at the Army. This had not happened even in the militancy years of the late '80s and the early '90s.

If we are not careful, there could be a lose-lose situation for all. As the flower of Kashmir's youth is mowed down, India will lose its democratic shine—ironically, under a leader who commands a bigger majority in parliament than any of his predecessors in a quarter-century. Or, is it the seemingly impregnable majority, which is leading this man into pathways of hubris, which clouds his reason?

It is evident there are four key differences between then—the first militancy, a quarter-century ago—and now. The first three concern the militants, the last the national political leadership. Together, they point to a worsened situation—one that will encourage Pakistan and its closest ally, China, to frame anti-India moves.

One, there is no more a fear factor in Kashmir. The weapons of the men in uniform are today up for snatching, as we saw in Anantnag last week with the CRPF. Earlier, weapons of only the J&K police used to be snatched. When the security forces did a cordon and search in the past, the villagers would run away out of fear, but not now.

Two, in the earlier militancy, young men gathered up gumption to cross the Line of Control to go into PoK for training at ISI-designated camps. Nowadays, arms training, and to an extent arms caches, are home-delivered. This has happened in the last three years, on Modi's watch.

Three, there is now no pro-independence party or faction left in the Kashmir Valley in any effective, real sense although Yasin Malik is still around. He and Mirwaiz Umar Farooq are obliged to kowtow to separatist stalwart Syed Ali Shah Geelani, the grandfather of all pro-Pakistan elements, considering the situation on the ground.

Four, and crucially, the present national leadership has allowed its regional ally PDP of Mufti to get discredited. But in an earlier period, Delhi tried to foster the regional Kashmiri partner, which was more in tune with local sensitivities. This gave elbow room to the Centre and the state government. That creative space, which afforded scope for governance ingenuity, has disappeared.

There is also an unconnected and extremely important fifth factor, namely, that until only a few months ago, many even among the most rabid Islamic Right in the Valley desired a dialogue with the Centre. Non-official interlocutors would be sometimes asked: "Do you have access to the PM's office and can you ask them to initiate talks? If you can't, why are you wasting time talking to us?" Perhaps the phase of asking such questions will soon be over.

Why is it necessary to have a continuous political conversation in the Kashmir context when Kashmir is an integral part of India? The answer is that this is a necessity flowing from a constitutional requirement.

Asian Age & The Deccan Chronicle, May 8, 2017

Uri Terror Attack: Of Little Real Consequence

The Uri terrorist attack from across the LOC on Sunday morning has two clear dimensions: one to do with the current turmoil in the Valley inspired by the pro-Pakistan constituencies; and the other that has all too conspicuous implications for the India-Pakistan dynamics ("relations" being too strong a word for now), and for the broader meaning of war and peace, especially in the backdrop of a strategic nuclear overhang.

On the first, the news so far is actually good. Ground reports—which Kashmir-datelined news stories have not yet reflected—suggest that there is no sense of thrill or excitement at an important army base being attacked by co-religionist irregular warriors from "the other side" who aid the "freedom struggle" and teach the "oppressor" a lesson from time to time.

In the volatile South Kashmir districts in today's context, the army has not yet seen it necessary to move in to contain the situation. This is suggestive of the fact that the situation needs watching but may be on the mend. Broadband Internet services that had been suspended were restored two days ago and have not been shut down again after Uri.

Can this change overnight if Pakistan shifts gears and instructs its sympathisers to seize the opportunity to re-double their efforts to harass the enemy through insurrectionary protest marches and similar instruments? Islamabad's aim, after all, is to seek to reassure the Kashmiri Muslim that it stands four-square behind their supposed aspirations, and a big proof of this is an attack on the army.

Conceivably, the situation could change therefore, and there could be a spurt in political activity by the pro-Pakistan elements. But this cannot be a qualitative change. The reason is that Pakistan's sympathisers have been at it way too long-three months since early July.

Using fear and threat as leverage, they rounded up the populace to do their bidding (ie. having to show up in staged marches and raise the Pakistan flag). But now ordinary folk are hurting. The peak business season is over and the tourism and the fruit industry have suffered in a way these haven't for a quarter century.

In other words, as a morale-booster the Uri attack has come late in the day. In that sense it is of little long-term consequence, although the aim of the planners would certainly have been to raise the tempo of the "insurrection", to make it look possibly worse than what the situation was in the early nineties in the high noon of Kashmiri militancy, and (with the smoking gun still smoking) to do a diplomatic carpet-bombing in UN General Assembly's tourist season when heads of state and government gather in New York.

This brings us to the second aspect relating to the Uri attack by Islamabad's militant proxies—that of exacting military revenge. From time to time, a perfectly normal case can be made to inflict punishment on Pakistan's military establishment, which has been cowardly and sneaky because it has been defeated on the battlefield over and over again, and in that process has frequently earned the wrath of its own people.

May be, war as a tactic of state to inflict at least a quarter century of peace on the Pakistan army (about the time taken for it to emotionally recoup from the trauma of yet another defeat), which has a massive chip on its shoulder in relation to India, should be planned for as an essential contingency of state. But war after Uri, which has failed to meet even short-term objectives of the highly militarised Pakistani state? This does seem incongruous.

Nevertheless, this is the language we hear in loud decibels from the Hindu Far Right. "For a tooth, the whole jaw" is an unfortunate example of this. Prime Minister Narendra Modi has said that the perpetrators of Uri "shall not go unpunished". Fortunately, he did not elaborate.

A miasma of mystery that leaves the adversary guessing is no bad thing. It also has the virtue of leaving all options on the table, to be used as and when needed by a self-confident state, in keeping with one's potential and the specific requirements of a given political moment. But Modi's cohorts, and quite possibly some of his top advisors too, appear innocent of the nuances and demands of state-craft.

There is a need to make a distinction between the Pathankot attack on January 2 this year and the attack on the administrative block of the brigade headquarters at Uri on September 18. The first was a distinct marker. It succeeded in its aim—designed doubtless by the Pakistan army—to disperse all efforts by the Indian side to obtain a state of normality with Pakistan, and putting paid to the desires of the civilian constituencies in that country. It was a defining moment in a sense. But no one spoke of going to war then.

Uri, unlike Pathankot, is but an episode in the Kashmir saga. It has neither strategic nor tactical significance in relation to Kashmir. In relation to Pakistan, its meaning can be made to look big or small, depending on the political need of the ruling establishment.

Economic Times, September 20, 2016

How to Take Kashmir off the Boil? Govt Must Advance Constitutional Reform

With respect to Kashmir, we are not near a watershed moment yet. But a strong potential for it exists if the Government of India can advance an agenda of constitutional reform for Kashmir as a quick follow-up to the recent two-day visit of an all-party delegation of MPs to the Valley.

Kashmiris make a valid criticism when they say that discussions following the massive 2010 disturbances yielded no shade of reform, although numerous ideas concerning the hues of autonomy, as well as specific economic needs of the different regions of the state of Jammu and Kashmir, were discussed through various forums.

Even so, ordinary folk had waited for the Parliamentary delegation with a sense of anticipation. Their revolt was against the callous disregard by the PDP-BJP state government of their economic, political and security needs, but they'd hoped fresh ideas would be thrown up when MPs from across the spectrum got to hear Kashmir speak in the context of today.

This was the message coming from the ground, even as protest rallies were being taken out in the villages. But the Hurriyat Conference, led by Syed Ali Shah Geelani, appears to have disregarded popular sentiment in rejecting the MPs' overtures for a worthwhile conversation.

Its stock in the Valley is expected to plunge further as a result. In a situation such as this, it will be plain foolishness for the Centre to take any steps that may help the Hurriyat leadership regain a modicum of public sympathy.

Reports suggest that the government may be contemplating tightening the screws on the leading lights of the Hurriyat, and that their security may be downgraded. Such optics to please the Hindu nationalist constituencies - to punish Geelani and others for showing the temerity to refuse talks with our MPs (this has been the running drumbeat of the ultra-nationalist sections of the television channels, for example) - can only boomerang on the government, and give the Hurriyat bosses a lease of life.

If the government really wishes to teach the separatists a lesson, it should make bold announcements in good faith, not contemplate revenge tactics. Just bear in mind that rejection of dialogue by the Hurriyat has not gone down well among ordinary people.

That said, it is everyone's right, including that of the Hurriyat leaders, to decline an invitation to converse. Besides - just think about it - the mandate of Hurriyat is to create problems for the Indian state, not solve them, especially when it is spearheaded by the most ardent pro-Pakistan leader in Kashmir.

The bulk of Kashmiri opinion does not look upon Pakistan favourably. And yet, a revolt of extraordinary proportions has rocked Kashmir. This is because ordinary people were extremely unhappy with the PDP-BJP government in the state.

It dashed their expectations and gave them next to nil relief in the aftermath of the flood of September 2014, the worst in recorded history, which had converted all of south Kashmir and most of the city of Srinagar into a gigantic lake.

Financial assistance from the Centre had been a key reason that the public had supported the PDP's joining hands with the Hindutva-oriented BJP. But instead of engaging in constructive politics in the Valley, the BJP component of the government - in order to shore up its image among its followers in the rest of the country - got into a series of pointless and dangerous communal diversions, such as beef and flag politics in the Valley, and pushed unwholesome ideas such as building ghettos for Kashmiri Pandits (when few Pandits wish to return to the valley). There were other Hindu communal interventions too.

At the same time as the politics was being mismanaged by the BJP, the security situation was also permitted to slide precipitously in a sign of irresponsible neglect by a government at the Centre whose leaders see themselves as ultra-nationalists. In 2016, the infiltration from Pakistan into Kashmir increased 200% over 2014, allowing an armed foreign terrorist contingent to burrow into Kashmir, and wait for an opportunity to strike.

The PDP watched the BJP's political gamesmanship helplessly, unable to force the saffron party back because its own legislators and ministers were loathe to let go of the loaves and fishes of office. Chief Minister Mehbooba Mufti had not bargained for this when she agreed to lead the government after weeks of hesitation following the death of her father, Mufti Mohammad Sayeed, in early 2016.

Hizbul Mujahideen commander Burhan Wani's killing was only a trigger. People erupted in spontaneous rebellion when it occurred. If that fateful encounter hadn't taken place, another inflection point is likely to have been discovered on the smallest pretext soon enough. Desperation had reached cracking point.

It is important to consider, though, that people were only resorting to marches in anger across south Kashmir, and in one instance, attacked a police station. The thoroughly organised stone-pelting brigade arrived on the scene only afterward, when friends of Pakistan in the Valley, a tiny but determined minority who are experts in propaganda and hit-and-run tactics, seized upon the public anger as a godsend, and then turned to manipulate the situation to their advantage.

It is important to separate the two manifestly different stages of the current revolt: the brief burst of spontaneous anger of the common folk in the first three days, and the calculated, choreographed and staged rebellion that subsequently took its place, with the ordinary rural people being pressurised to join out of a sense of deep insecurity and fear, so great is the feeling of dread the pro-Pakistan elements generate among the people.

This derives from the manner in which the Jamat-e-Islami cadres especially went about dealing with those who crossed their ideological path during the intense militancy years of 1989-93.

It has now been two months, and the stone-pelting has not stopped. The industry just doesn't seem to stop churning out more stones. Such a prolonged protest lock-down of the Valley has not been seen before, and the end seems nowhere in sight.

Especially in the south Kashmir districts, but also in the northern parts of the Valley, marching through villages by people in their hundreds with the Pakistan flag aloft has become an everyday sight. Interestingly, all the flags flown at these rallies appear identical to the observer, as though sourced from the same tailor across the border or some suitable quarters in New Delhi, and appear to have materialised overnight as though under a well-devised plan. There are no signs of any being home-stitched by unpractised hands in rural Kashmir.

It is now becoming plain to many in the Valley that the unprecedented hyper-activity of the pro-Pakistan sections is traceable to Prime Minister Narendra Modi's Independence Day speech naming Balochistan and PoK for human rights violations by Pakistan. It is a sort of revenge extraordinary that we are witnessing. Given the geography, Islamabad is intervening with ferocity after it dedicated its own Independence Day this year to the cause of Kashmir.

From available accounts, the common Kashmiri is keen to return to normal life as quickly as possible, but is virtually being held hostage by pro-Pakistan contingents. Only the government possesses the resources and the political ability and flexibility to bail him out of his present misery.

And in the situation that exists, this is possible only

through a political initiative of an entirely new type - and not through an extensive crackdown by the security forces that will show Pakistan's backers in poor light in the eyes of the people.

When the ruler of Jammu and Kashmir, Maharaja Hari Singh, signed the Instrument of Accession with India in October 1947, he had ceded to New Delhi only the portfolios of defence, foreign affairs and communications. Much else has come under Delhi's domain since then. The titles of constitutional o□ces - "Sadr-e-Riyasat" for the Governor and "Prime Minister" for the Chief Minister - also vanished with time, though that was not part of the deal.

Over the decades, this entire process has caused intense heartburn in the Valley, accompanied by a sense of inadequacy and the feeling of being slighted as a people. The time has come to end the alienation and set the record straight, to give the people of Kashmir the option to take only those laws of the Republic of India that they wish to in their own wisdom, and dispense with others.

Catch News, Sepetember 18, 2016

A New Start in Kashmir

Above all, what afflicts the people of Kashmir Valley is a sense of humiliation. This has built up over the decades. This is what Pakistan, the separatists and the small but ever-present pro-Pakistan constituency, always seek to exploit. But so must all democrats be concerned about this deeply sensitive issue if they are serious about being democrats—party colours don't matter.

And this is what the all-party delegation of our MPs led by home minister Rajnath Singh should keep in view in Srinagar on Sunday, and try to offer reasonable assurances that steps can be taken to restore Kashmir's hurt pride.

The MPs' delegation should know that ordinary people in the Valley are looking to their arrival with hope, notwithstanding the curfews and protests, some of the latter being a put up job. In truth, everyone is by now mentally exhausted—not just the security forces. The unprecedented shutdown is nearly two months old.

"Development" and "defeat of poverty" are always important. But these can't be equated with people's pride and sense of belonging. In any case, our MPs should be aware that Kashmir Valley is among the economically better off places in the country, thanks to Sheikh Abdullah's "land to the tiller" programme which came under his Naya Kashmir or 'New Kashmir' initiative guided by his Leftist friends back in the day.

We must also bear in mind that only the Government of India can bring back sanity, not the chief minister or the 15th

Corps commander. As for the separatists, they revel in seeing bridges burn. Some of them are "naysayers" by conviction as they'd like Kashmir to join Pakistan, some take money to speak negative language, and some are genuinely afraid of being shot dead on instruction from "the other side" if they show the smallest inclination to talk to New Delhi.

Several prominent personalities have thus been eliminated, and this makes the fear real. In any case, New Delhi alone—not just the Government of India but also our Parliament—has the power to make a difference.

The key separatists are likely to engage in baiting talk but do little to alleviate the miseries of the people. They are not in the business to look for solutions. They have not been elected, and are therefore not answerable to the people. They are there to stoke the fires.

The more miserable and alienated the people, the more the separatists prosper politically, and derive associated benefits. Remember, there is a proxy war on. Politics under the shadow of the gun is what we are condemned to negotiate.

The Kashmiris understand this. They are among the politically shrewdest people anywhere and perfectly capable of speaking in nuanced code language, and are not given only to exaggerated chest- beating and shrieking, which is alas what comes across on television screens as journalism—including in Kashmir—these days which privileges drama over substance.

But because the people of Kashmir are not naive, they know when New Delhi is serious, and when it makes meaningless noises. If the Centre is serious, the people will lose no time in putting the separatists in their place.

Atal Behari Vajpayee as Prime Minister struck a chord in the Valley because he did not speak only of "jamhooriyat" (democracy) but also "Kashmiriyat" and "insaniyat" (humanism). No one had done this before. "Kashmiriyat" addressed identity issues, including those relating to politics. "Insaniyat" took care of matters relating to violence and related abuses (from the side of the State and the militants in the insurgency years of 1989-93).

Speaking in the impersonalised categories of democracy, development, integration and unity, or talking up the clichés of confidence, trust and healing touch, would have set Mr Vajpayee on a barren course. These have become vacuous phrases from an unproductive past. But mechanically repeating or rehashing the Vajpayee vocabulary today won't do either.

Before Mr Vajpayee, his predecessor P.V. Narasimha Rao had said, "The sky is the limit" for Kashmir's autonomy within the outlines of the Indian Constitution. The late PM's words are also recalled in the Valley. But for the people of Kashmir, the uplifting language of the Rao era did not leave the page on which it was written.

This is where this all-party MPs' team can make a contribution. To begin with, it can advance an idea which is full of powerful symbolism and seeks to directly address the "humiliation" issue—that calling the J&K governor "Sadr-e-Riyasat", and the Chief Minister "Prime Minister", as in the old days, can be revived.

Such nomenclature remained long in use after the last Kashmir Maharaja, Hari Singh, who wished to remain independent of both India and Pakistan but found it expedient to sign the Instrument of Accession with India when Pakistan sent raiders and invaders into the Valley in October 1947, was obliged to demit office.

When Kashmir formally agreed to be incorporated into the territory of India, it was also agreed that the J&K constitution and flag would remain in use, and this agreement has been duly honoured. So, what's wrong with the recall of names of prominent constitutional positions.

If this happens, a frisson of excitement will course through the whole Valley. Also, in PoK and Gilgit-Baltistan, the example will put enormous pressure on the Pakistani authorities who have made these regions an inconsequential fiefdom of a militarised State bordering on Islamism.

At the time of accession, Maharaja Hari Singh had agreed only to surrender foreign affairs, defence and communication to New Delhi. It is time to institute a commission to study which laws passed by parliament can be adopted by the J&K Assembly for implementation, and whether any should be deleted. The Indian Constitution and our laws are among the most progressive in the world. Kashmir itself may voluntarily choose many or most of our laws—such as those relating to the judiciary, labour, women and children, or the right to information.

In real terms, measures such as these do underscore the idea of "autonomy", and India can take up the matter internally. Talks with Pakistan—of the kind that PM Manmohan Singh developed to link J&K with PoK through trade—are not needed for this.

Asian Age & The Deccan Chronicle , September 4, 2016

It is Pakistan's Advantage When Delhi is Not Savvy Enough to Open Lines of Communication with People in Kashmir Valley

It is advantage Pakistan when New Delhi is not savvy enough to open lines of communication with its own people in the Kashmir Valley. That is exactly what gives Islamabad every leeway it needs to make trouble for us and, in the process, give the people in Kashmir a taste of hell.

This is what happened in the high noon of Pakistan-inspired militancy during 1990-94. The Indian state was pushed really hard, and had to shoot its way out of a corner. And, especially in rural Kashmir, nobody's home was safe.

Women became a special target of the 'friends' from across the LOC who came to 'liberate' Kashmiri Muslims. People remember those times with a shudder and a curse.

Cadres of the National Conference were being hanged from the nearest tree by Pakistan's agents. Congress supporters were on the run. Social and physical infrastructure was destroyed with deliberation to hurt India.

The Jammu and Kashmir Liberation Front (JKLF), which called for an 'independent' Kashmir and did not favour merger with Pakistan, was targeted and its men killed by Pakistan's accomplices under a carefully worked ISI plan, and implemented by militant outfits that drew their philosophical, political, military and financial sustenance from Islamabad.

It was a truly bad and dangerous period of history. No

Kashmiri wishes to return to that hell. Does New Delhi?

In the 16 months that the PDP-BJP government has been in place, the Centre has not initiated a single move to open an avenue of constructive politics with the Kashmiri people. In its place, there have been egregious moves to communalise the political sphere. Beef politics was accorded high place.

After some Kashmiri students at the Regional Engineering College in Srinagar raised pro-Pakistan slogans, the on-campus Kashmir Police was displaced by the CRPF —as if to signal a 'Hindu' force had marched in. India's name suffered as a result.

It seemed that the BJP, having won all its seats in J&K assembly from Jammu, was seeking to cater to its Hindu constituency exclusively, instead of thinking big as an all-India party of all Indians, including the people of Kashmir.

To worsen matters, the relief provided by the central government for the floods of September 2014 that drowned Srinagar and all of South Kashmir was a measly Rs 2,000 crore, when it should have been nearer Rs 1lakh crore.

Thus, through our own ineptness, we handed Islamabad all the aces, which it will now try to play. Let's bear in mind that the mood in the Valley was already sour and alienated before the killing of Hizbul Mujahideen commander Burhan Wani by security forces on July 8.

Wani's charisma owed to the spread of his profile through the social media, and his elimination produced a backlash of protest across Kashmir, of such magnitude that about 50 civilians, including children, were killed in firing by the security grid.

Scores of protesters lost their eyesight due to pellet guns obviously fired above waist level, about which questions should be asked and punishments meted out at the command level—for the failure to gauge the impact of an action on citizens and its likely social and political fallout, which in this case Pakistan will seek to exploit.

Available reports indicate that Pakistan was unlikely to

have been involved in instigating the first rounds of the recent violence—as the Centre insists—and only came in a little later when it realised that the Indians had goofed up bad. If this is not understood, our tactics and strategy would be misdirected.

The first step: communicate with the alienated in Kashmir. This has been done before.

Pakistan typically panics when New Delhi is able to speak to Kashmiris, and does its worst to sabotage a step in that direction. We saw this when Prime Minister Atal Bihari Vajpayee did the unthinkable. He paved the way for talks with a section of the Hizbul Mujahideen, the pro-Pakistan militant outfit.

Majeed Dar, its most important military leader, was brought on board for a conversation. The ISI had him killed in his home. That was the level of Pakistan's insecurity when India meant business.

Economic Times, August, 6, 2016

Kashmir Unrest: How BJP-PDP have Made a Complete Mess

When it comes to the deadly street violence in Kashmir following the killing of young Hizbul Mujahideen commander Burhan Wani, two features stand out. One, while there was furious stone-pelting by mobs across the valley, no demands accompanied the violent protests. Public agitations in Kashmir, even violent ones, have generally had a theme, and have been accompanied by a set of demands, as the episodes of mass unrest in 2008 and 2010 show.

The absence of a specific core issue can raise uncomfortable questions, as it is in some ways reminiscent of the militancy years between 1989 and 1994. At that time, the alienation at the popular level had built up to a febrile pitch following the rigged state election of 1987. With Pakistan helping to establish the militancy, and support it with weapons, money, propaganda and personnel, the militants believed the iron was hot and they struck hard.

That confluence of circumstances has not again been replicated. However, what's worrying is that a mood of insurgency - something which sways ordinary people at a broader level, and not support for just terrorism - seems to have been evolving of late, especially since the PDP-BJP coalition government came into being in early 2015.

On more than one occasion in the past eight to ten months, particularly in the southern part of the valley, the general area where Wani was killed, villagers, including womenfolk, have come out to form a barrier, deliberately impeding operations by the security forces against terrorists, including Pakistani infiltrators.

The disenchantment among the people and sense of being let down has been gathering steam on account of the many failures of the state government and the Centre in a short span of time.

To begin with, the massive Kashmir flood of September 2014, which engulfed Srinagar almost in its entirety, elicited from the Centre a less than modest support by way of relief of Rs 2,000 crore when reasonable estimates were pointing to the need for about Rs 1,00,000 crore.

The developing discontent makes New Delhi's case unconvincing that the recent violence has been the handiwork of Pakistan, although Islamabad does seek to fish in troubled waters, and finds support in the valley from those owing allegiance to the Jamaat-e-Islami ideology and harbouring sympathy for the Hizbul Mujahideen, frequently described as the militant arm of the Jamaat.

Nevertheless, the trigger for the current unrest appears to have been local. Islamabad came in with diplomatic and propaganda support, describing the slain popular local militant Wani as a 'martyr'—rather than 'terrorist'—and Pakistan Prime Minister Nawaz Sharif asserting that Kashmir would accede to Pakistan, but that was days after the violence broke out.

The second noteworthy feature of the recent protests is the clamping of unrelenting curfew across the valley for over a fortnight.

Usually the authorities offer brief breaks in the restraint hours to allow people to procure essentials - medicines, baby foods, perishable items. Shops open and shut quickly, and people can stir out. Such moves permit psychological relief, and work as a safety valve. That crutch was not on offer this time around.

The matter was compounded with the separatist leaders too calling for a valley-wide 'hartal' or general strike when the curfew was already in effect, in a self-serving way seeking to create the impression that people were heeding their call for protest against 'Indian occupation' and its consequences.

They needed to posture because the action of the violent mobs pelting stones at the security forces generally appeared to be spontaneous in the beginning, unlike in 2010, when the same tactic had been well orchestrated.

Maintaining protracted valley-wide curfew without any relief to ordinary people for 16 or 17 consecutive days appears to have fed the sense of Kashmir being rudely disregarded by the government in a time of acute psychological distress - exactly the narrative that played out at the time of the terrible flood in 2014, although on that occasion state government offices were themselves under water and unable to render meaningful assistance.

After the extreme militancy years of the early nineties, veterans are hard put to recall curfew restrictions with no breaks.

There are three segments of opinion in the valley - favouring 'azadi' or having an independent state, remaining with India, and merging with Pakistan. The last option is widely thought to be the least popular.

Nevertheless, pro-Pakistan elements may be said to be the best organised and ready for street action (and also a degree of violence). In the public mind, this is because they have the backing of 'the gun' - the terrorist outfits sheltering in PoK or in Pakistan proper.

Even so, the pro-Pakistan sections pick on issues to agitate about that are likely to have a broad appeal, and are not necessarily tied to the objectives of a particular militant group or party. It is noteworthy in this context that the recent violence was to protest the killing of a commander of Hizbul Mujahideen, not by a long chalk Kashmir's most popular militant outfit.

True, Wani had gained popularity on account of his use of social media to connect with fellow Kashmiris, especially the youth. This made him a household name, and his death became a personally felt experience for many. But in political terms, protesting in his name amounted to rallying to a pro-Pakistan cause, not a common valley occurrence.

Contacts in rural Kashmir now report hearing whispers to the effect that, for their own safety, people should stop moving about freely, as this could be the return of 'the bad old days' - when pro-Pakistan militants roamed freely in the villages, extracting revenge from the pro-azadi elements and those backing mainline parties. The corollary of this is the return of 'crackdowns' and cordon-and-search operations, a hated prospect.

This is a terrible, morale-sapping state of affairs. How has this come about? Evidently, the PDP-BJP coalition government has paid little attention to governance and constructive politics and engagement with the people.

The BJP, in particular, has stuck mostly to keeping alive a 'Hindu nationalist' agenda and refrain - through the beef narrative, the high-decibel propaganda about building of secure housing clusters for Kashmiri pandits who left the valley years ago and show no interest in returning, and the hyping up of the incident in the Regional Engineering College in Srinagar earlier this year when some Kashmiri students raised pro-Pakistan slogans. And, there is not much to show on the positive side.

The PDP, which grew as a 'soft-separatist' regional party, has simply been unable to resist the BJP's onslaught because its legislators seem bent on wanting to enjoy the loaves and fishes of office, and have no desire to rock the boat by interrogating the BJP's political stance.

The government's lack of concern about issues that matter to the people has had a negative fallout on the security front, as well as in the domain of politics, which, in Kashmir, is crucially important on account of the ever-present Pakistan factor. The infiltration of armed jihadist irregulars from the Pakistan side has reportedly increased 200% this year already.

In the area of broader politics, not even a half-hearted attempt has been made by the present government to re-start conversations with the civil society and others on matters relating to issues such as 'autonomy', given Kashmir's specific history.

After the militancy years, then-Prime Minister PV Narasimha Rao had got political and electoral processes re-started by undertaking just such an exercise, which gained considerable traction under PM Atal Bihari Vajpayee afaterward.

Momentum was retained with PM Manmohan Singh setting up interlocutors for Kashmir, and opening a dialogue on Kashmir with Pakistan that came close to fruition, going by the accounts of participants in the process on both sides.

The present situation looks difficult and volatile - with a communal narrative driving the agenda from one side and causing widespread resentments in the valley. The other side has responded with the witch's brew of similar potency or worse.

Catch News, August 2, 2016

Playing Dangerous Game in Kashmir

When Pakistan tries to keep the pot boiling in Kashmir, its malicious intent must be countered with vigour. It is an unsatiated state that is trying to grab the territory, using the bogus argument that it has a proprietary right over a Muslim-majority area.

But what's to be said when India—on account of the maladroit actions of its government—ends up creating an unstable and volatile situation in Kashmir, playing right into Islamabad's hands.

The recent Valley-wide violence in Kashmir erupted after the security forces killed a young commander of the pro-Pakistan terror outfit Hizbul Mujahideen, Burhan Wani, who had gained Valley-wide popularity through the clever use of social media, a propaganda tool used to great effect by jihadi outfits worldwide, particularly the Islamic State and Al Qaeda.

On this basis the BJP, which runs the Centre and is in a coalition government with Mehbooba Mufti's People's Democratic Party in Kashmir, is trying to project itself as a political force that is alive to its "nationalist" responsibility. It has exchanged hostile words with Pakistan and has stuck to the narrative that the violent unrest seen in the Valley since Wani's death on July 8 was the handiwork of Pakistan and its proxies.

This is an artificial narrative. It is also an artifice to camouflage the communal agenda unleashed in the Valley whose bitter fruit the country is now harvesting. It is an entirely self-serving and inaccurate projection to conceal how matters have shaped in Kashmir since the PDP-BJP government came into being in March 2015.

Looking at the facts, it is evident that the initial violence after Wani's killing was spontaneous, a *sui generis* development. Islamabad began to meddle through propaganda interventions, and fish in troubled waters in other ways, after the lapse of a few days—not right away.

While misguiding the country, the Centre and the state government are refusing to see that what's confronting us is a pervasive mood of popular dissatisfaction in Kashmir that is akin to the rumblings of an incipient insurgency.

If the causes of alienation that has built up in recent times are not addressed, and strong-arm methods continue to be used against the populace as a whole, instead of taking the bull by the horns and getting down to serious political engagement, we cannot get the tactics right to deal with the situation.

A lot of hope had been invested in the PDP-BJP government by the people of Kashmir but these were dashed to the ground by the constant communal needling that the BJP has engaged in since coming into government in the state, instead of seeking to build political capital for itself in the Muslim-majority Valley in the way that Atal Behari Vajpayee- also from the BJP- did as Prime Minister.

The BJP's political campaigns in the state (under Modi) took care to focus attention on themes that were aimed to show that the so-called Hindu interests would be highlighted.

A perverse reading was sought to be imposed that defending the perceived Hindu interests in J&K automatically meant defending the country's interests—in fact, playing on the subliminal thought among many that Hindus and Muslims have separate interests. (This is exactly the way of thinking that brought about Pakistan.)

Beef politics was kept alive for weeks. When a misguided "beef party" was held by a Valley MLA, Engineer Rashid, to get even with the BJP for its high-decibel cow politics in the rest of the country, the saffron party's state bosses saw red. No one told them that the episode involving the independent MLA was a bait and that the Kashmiri Muslim wasn't even a beef-eater traditionally.

The pseudo-politics of nationalism alos came to be played out in J&K, taking off from developments in JNU in the course of which Union home minister Rajnath Singh made an assertion that was shown to be false—that the involvement of a Kashmiri young man at a JNU protest action was inspired by Pakistan's Lashkar-e-Tayyaba mentor Hafiz Sayed.

In this period, the shouting of pro-Pakistan slogans by some Kashmiri boys at the Regional Engineering College in Srinagar came to the fore. All hell broke loose. The event was converted into a Hindu-Muslim issue. The Kashmir police was substituted on the campus by the Central Reserve Police Force, as if the latter was a force that reflected "Hindu India".

Besides corrupting and polluting the political atmosphere, developments such as these harmed not just the Centre's but India's reputation in the Valley, where only a small section of opinion is deemed to be pro-Pakistan.

All meaningful work was neglected while politics around an explicit communal agenda dominated the landscape. It appeared that since the BJP had won all its seats from Hindu-dominated Jammu, the party was trying to pander to the "Hindu vote" in Jammu.

Mufti and her party became worried onlookers, as disgust with the BJP began to take hold amongst the populace, and with her for allying with the BJP. This began to get translated into an anti-India sentiment which was sought to be fanned by the separatist quarters.

Massive floods had ravaged Kashmir, particularly the ancient and throbbing city of Srinagar and all of South Kashmir, in September 2014, months before the election that brought the PDP-BJP coalition. An important consideration for the PDP going with the BJP was the expectation that financial assistance for flood relief would flow if the regional party was aligned with the Centre. But a less than paltry Rs 2,000 crores has been allotted so far to mitigate flood-related damage, when the need was for around Rs 100,000 crores.

The mood among the people had turned grim and sullen long before the Burhan Wani killing, which as an event acted as a catalyst—no more. Besides doing little on the development front, the government failed on the political and security front.

The Pakistani infiltration this year is reportedly 200 per cent higher than in 2014, and there has been no move from the Centre to take the Valley people into a fold of constructive politics—a trend tha was seen since the time of Prime Minister P.V. Narasimha Rao. It is dangerous that Kashmir has been left adrift at a time when China and Pakistan have been holding joint patrols in the Pakistan-occupied Kashmir (PoK) area.

Asian Age & The Deccan Chronicle, August 1, 2016

India and the World

Big Power, Big Fail

China scuttling a move in the UN Security Council on Wednesday to have a key Pakistani terrorist guru, the Jaish-e-Mohammed chief Masood Azhar, listed as a "global terrorist". This is an expression of surprising agnosticism on questions of war and peace, given the specific context in which Azhar was being sought to be punished by the international community.

Such an act of sheer irresponsibility by a major power raises the question of its suitability to play a constructive part in regional and world affairs, including in Afghanistan (which borders China and Pakistan), where a peace deal with the Taliban is being sought to be negotiated in preparation for the departure of US troops from that country.

Using its position as a veto-wielding UNSC member, Beijing had bailed out Azhar in 2009, 2016 and 2017. But this time around, given the background in which Azhar was given a life-line, China's action has the potential to instigate Pakistan—and the thousands of trained anti-India terrorists who harbour in that country- to continually engage in brinkmanship in its India dynamics, unconcerned about regional peace and stability.

After the JeM mounted a terrorist attack in Pulwama, Jammu and Kashmir, last month, and New Delhi's request to Islamabad to act against the outfit fell on deaf ears, the Indian Air Force bombed a suspected JeM training centre inside Pakistan. In response, Pakistani planes crossed Indian airspace and dropped ordnance inside a military compound near the border before being chased away.

Fortunately, no real damage was done, or the strategic calculus could have taken on an unpredictable and undesirable turn. But it was a tense military moment. The use of air power can have escalatory consequences. No two countries with proven nuclear weapons have engaged in an air battle inside the territory of one of them before.

Without losing time, two sets of actors worked behind the scenes to calm things down and stanch escalation fears. Leading western powers took the matter to the UNSC to chasten Azhar. His outfit has already been proscribed by the UN. So, it was logical that international restraints be placed on Azhar also. This was not an action against Pakistan, China's "all-weather" and "iron" friend, but against a leading non-state actor who routinely wreaks havoc inside India.

And, still, Beijing could not bring itself to back the move. It can now be safely said that China has flunked the terrorism test.

China was the only holdout on the Azhar issue in the UNSC. The resolution to list the terrorist was authored by France, the US, and Britain. Among its co-sponsors were not only key Europeans, Australia and Japan, but also South Asian Association for Regional Cooperation (Saarc) members Bhutan, Bangladesh and the Maldives.

Thus, today China presents the picture of a brazen state that has no compunction in giving moral and political solace to a dangerous non-state actor, not unlike Pakistan with which its friendship, in its own words, is "as high as the mountains, as deep as the seas".

The second set of actors that tried to play a helpful role in the crisis set off by the action of a terror group was from the Gulf region. Saudi Arabia, which carries weight with Pakistan since it bankrolls the latter heavily, was active at the highest level with supportive counsel.

In a first, the United Arab Emirates (UAE), which earlier this month hosted the ministerial meeting of the Organisation of Islamic Cooperation (OIC) in Abu Dhabi, specially invited

India's external affairs minister Sushma Swaraj to be a "guest of honour". This was patently a gesture meant to cool the India-Pakistan environment- for, shortly afterward, the OIC went back to taking its decades-old standard line on Kashmir, which is to criticise India. China remained impervious to the wide import of these developments and the concern in international circles about nuclear-armed countries taking the first steps toward conflict.

It is no surprise that Beijing should wholly disregard the spirit of the deliberations at the "informal summit" at Wuhan in China between Prime Minister Narendra Modi and President Xi Jinping in April 2018, which was meant to normalise frayed Sino-Indian ties in the wake of the Doklam border crisis.

The third paragraph of the statement issued by the ministry of external affairs on the Wuhan talks, issued on April 28 last year, speaks of the two countries "respecting each other's sensitivities, concerns and aspirations". This was not to be. India frequently refers to the "Wuhan spirit", taking Chinese commitments too seriously.

A subsequent paragraph reiterated the "resolute opposition" of the leaders "to terrorism in all its forms and manifestations". Modi and Xi also "committed themselves to cooperate on counter-terrorism."

It is evident that China's massive infrastructure investments—which will culminate in a naval base in Pakistan's Gwadar port—pre-dispose it to unmindfully back Pakistan. But, at the UNSC, the issue was that of punishing a key terrorist whose outfit routinely kills people in India. Evidently, Beijing's strategic disposition to contain India with Pakistan's help, even through the instrumentality of terrorism, has not dimmed. But this is a dangerous game.

Published 15 March, 2019, Economic Times

It's Too Early to Talk of a Modi-Imran Entente

It is quite remarkable how Prime Minister Narendra Modi and Pakistan's presumptive PM Imran Khan have hit upon the same slogan to pitch to their respective countries. Modi doesn't tire talking of "New India" while the Pakistan leader says it in Hindi/Urdu: "Naya Pakistan!" Are they similar in outlook? Will they be on the same wave-length when it comes to bilateral relations?

The questions are premature. Much would depend on how Khan copes as a politician in government, one holding the highest civilian office, especially in relation to the army, since in Pakistan it is the Army that matters most. And specifically in Khan's case, it is thought the military is the power behind the throne.

There are other considerations too. As a politician Khan's popularity has been rising over the years, and yet he needed the unmistakeable push the army gave him inn order to succeed. But he is not the only one the army has lately promoted.

Extremists and terrorists were made to run in the July 25 election in the military's effort to "mainstream" them. To a man, they lost. And yet, as an acute Indian observer of Pakistan, Tilak Devasher, a former senior officer of the cabinet secretariat whose 2016 book *Pakistan: Courting the Abyss* drew high praise from leading Pakistanis, said at a public form recently, "Though the extremists lost, they have been mainstreamed. They can wear party colours. The Army has succeeded in its objective."

Clearly, the terrorists can now be legitimate political operatives assembled under various party flags. They will, in fact, be the army's political storm-troopers and act as a forceful check on the incoming PM, should he begin to develop ideas of his own.

Whether Mr. Khan turns out to be like Modi or not, in his background, temperament and capability (in very different fields), he could bear comparison to the dodgy but brilliant- and ill-fated- Zulfikar Ali Bhutto. ZAB had an advantage over Khan. Until he himself created his nemesis, General Zia, for a long time he was dealing with an army that was mired in uncertainties and, after the 1971 defeat and the creation of Bangladesh, faced demoralisation. Even so, ZAB's approach is instructive.

In his just published *Pakistan: At the Helm*, Devasher writes: "Bhutto seemed determined to get into power, by hook or by crook....On one occasion (he) told Asghar Khan in 1970, 'We can rule together.' When Asghar Khan asked about his programme after coming into power, Bhutto chuckled and his reply was honest, though shocking to the air marshal. He said, "The programme is to rule. The people are stupid and I know how to fool them. I will have the "danda" (rod) in my hand and no one will be able to remove us for twenty years."

"Once entrenched in power, Bhutto systematically moulded state institutions to his will. In the process they were badly damaged and the state suffered the consequences. As Jamsheed Marker notes, the judiciary was made subservient, the powerful civil service was ruined with the introduction of the Lateral Entry Scheme that brought in party activists."

Khan has a far more confident Army to deal with than ZAB did. Still, how he navigates his way through the labyrinth will be interesting to watch. The first priority for PM Imran Khan will be to deal with the huge financial debt imposed upon Pakistan by China's special 'aid' funnelled for the China-Pakistan Economic Corridor (CPEC).

The Americans have said they'd use their influence in the

IMF to prevent a bailout package that would, in effect, fund China. If Khan is able to work out something favourable with the US, he'd have better standing in the country and some leeway with the military.

Optics matter, after all. For the Pakistan military, a civilian head of government is a necessity to sustain the appearance that Pakistan is at least half a democracy. Finding international aid for dictatorships gets difficult. And this need of the Army may give the PM a degree of latitude.

Kashmir and other issues come only later in priority. In fact, to balance Khan- especially if he is being successful- the army can keep up the terrorism pressure in Kashmir. This is a clever way to keep the newly mainstreamed elements happy. It is therefore just as well that foreign leaders are not being invited for Khan's inaugural. The ground is hardly ready for Modi to visit.

His external exuberance exhibited in December 2015, when he surprised then Pakistan PM Nawaz Sharief by turning up at his door uninvited in Lahore, had terrible consequences. It wasn't factored in by the Indians that the generals might disapprove.

The Modi gesture may have caused the feeling in the Pakistan army that the civilians were running away with too much leeway. This sense may have been reinforced as the previous year Sharief had, off his own bat, accepted the invitation to attend Modi's swearing-in ceremony in May, 2014. The retribution was swift in the form of the Pathankot attack. The relationship went into a downward spiral.

After the Pathankot and Uri attacks in 2016, New Delhi orchestrated a boycott of the 19th SAARC summit in Pakistan. With the exceptional success of the move, the Pakistan Army would always be left wondering whether invitees would show up if India was again a no-show, in case South Asian leaders were invited for Khan's inauguration.

There were thus good reasons for Modi not to visit Pakistan at the present juncture, seen from both India's perspective and Pakistan's. But there is also another very important consideration-Kashmir.

Kashmir is not quiet. There is obviously a huge and continuing Pakistani role, going back decades, but of late we have botched it real bad, politically. Arguably, there has not before been greater alienation at the popular level in the valley. Staunch supporters of Kashmir's integration with India, along with autonomy, have been pushed on the back foot. There can't be a worse time to talk Kashmir with Pakistan.

Modi did the right thing in phoning Khan to congratulate him and express a desire for improvement in relations. Not doing so after an election would have been churlish. On Thursday, Pakistan formally acknowledged the Indian leader's gesture and expressed a similar hope. Both sides kept it at the level of generalities. This is just as well for now. We can pick up the pieces once the situation in the valley improves.

Asian Age & The Deccan Chronicle, August 7, 2018

4 Yrs of Self-inflicted Wounds, An Era of Banality

As soon as Prime Minister Narendra Modi arrived on the scene, many in India associated with professional diplomacy, and taking a cue from them the broad foreign policy-security establishment circuit (including the think tank crowd and journalists, especially television pundits), began to anticipate a new dawn in this country's relations with the world.

What this upbeat assessment was based on was not clear, but everyone seemed awestruck by the PM's apparent energy as the new man in charge rushed from country to country, hugging world leaders and making anodyne speeches at Indian diaspora jamborees—of which the show at the Madison Square Garden in New York was typical—got together by the Vishwa Hindu Parishad. Aided by a swooning and chauvinistic Indian visual media, a foreign affairs rock star had been born.

But this was no Metternich, Churchill, Kissinger, Nehru, Zhou Enlai, Lee Kuan Yew or Nelson Mandela—stalwarts who had a conception of world affairs and a strategic vision, in addition to the material, moral or intellectual means to deploy to realise their vision, as well as the hallmarks of a teacher in their own time and afterward.

Four years since Modi's advent, as the country slips into election mode and groans and grunts of disapproval are becoming audible around the country, it is not out of place to ask where the foreign policy manoeuvres of the "strong" leader, with a majority of his own in parliament, have led us, and what laurels these have brought. Professional diplomats who once sang the leader's praise are today gobsmacked as questions fly in all directions.

The stalwarts of the past did not speak words of self-praise, but Modi did nothing but that as he flew around the world in designer jackets, uttering truths grown in his own kitchen garden.

His most profound sentences began and ended with the claim of him being the first Indian leader to land in such and such place in 10 or 20 or three years. In Canada, the self-advertisement was shown to be short on the truth. At any rate, it is not clear what has been gained from those visits. Nor did the PM bother checking if there was a reason why his predecessors had not been to a particular place.

In Kathmandu, the Indian PM strutted around the famous Pashupatinath temple dressed as the Hindu pope. In Lahore, he was the sari salesman bearing gifts for Nawaz Sharif's mother. In Ahmedabad, he was the boatman on the waterfront for Xi Jinping even as Chinese soldiers were busy trespassing into perceived Indian territory in disputed border areas. Modi the Innocent thought "charm" of this variety constituted the very essence of the diplomatic game. When it came to America, the PM was "aye, aye, sir!" whether it was Obama or Trump.

The pitiful results of these exertions lie scattered all around us. India's neighbourhood is practically in revolt against New Delhi. Forget "Muslim Pakistan", "Hindu Nepal" is telling Modi to get lost. China has hinted that India cannot afford another Doklam crisis as that might entail having to deal simultaneously with Beijing and Islamabad.

New Delhi's historical friend Moscow, which was the bulwark against anti-India Western manoeuvres on Kashmir in the UN Security Council, now openly flaunts its relations with China as well as Pakistan. It is this which has sent New Delhi diving to buy a consignment of S-400 missiles from Russia, in the process getting the Americans uptight.

No matter which way one cuts it, India's foreign policy under Modi leads to questions and no answers. In the months that remain, the peacock may dance but there will be no rain. For the first time since 1947, India's foreign policy efforts lack a national consensus; indeed, a conscious effort has been mounted from the heart of the policy establishment—the PMO—to chest-thump solely in order to denigrate parliamentary opponents.

A video of the so-called "surgical strike" against Pakistan—which has proved to be of no deterrence value in fighting terrorism or against Pakistani incursions or ceasefire violations in Kashmir—was yet again wheeled out recently as a gift to certain television stations to drum up pro-government propaganda in the run-up to the national election and the clutch of state polls that precede it.

This act will ensure that the present regime will remain incapacitated from pursuing a meaningful Pakistan policy that has the nation's backing. And, if there is no consensus on our Pakistan and China policies, which are among our most pressing international concerns, can we even say a foreign policy exists?

On an ultra-sensitive question like Kashmir, which draws international attention like flies are drawn to a pot of honey, the Modi government has ensured that its policy efforts elicit the deepest national cynicism, and produce despair. There is just no national unity as the regime goes about on a campaign of political abuse and vilification of regional Kashmir parties as well as national opponents.

On Kashmir, it was lack of policy direction and alertness on the part of the foreign policy establishment—whether residing in the external affairs ministry or the PMO—that the report of the UN Human Rights Council hit us smack in the eye and no one saw it coming. This has handed Pakistan and the Kashmiri extremists' propaganda for a generation against which the government can do little. Who is answerable—the PM or his external affairs minister?

Before Narendra Modi became PM, he had no international exposure as such. Of course, he had the worldview of the RSS whose brightest postulate—deriving from the exclamations of its leader Mohan Bhagwat—is the curious demand that the world must acknowledge India as the "vishwa guru" or teacher to the world. Do we laugh at this, or cry?

As the election approaches, it will be interesting to see what new facts are manufactured to make the Modi foreign policy look grand, and mighty and powerful, and how the perception is managed to secure narrow, personal ends of the leader without doing a thing for the country.

If it was ever true that India's foreign policy sank to the lowest depths of ordinariness, it is today. We have been witness to an era of banality and self-inflicted wounds.

Asian Age & The Deccan Chronicle, July 2, 2018

The China-Pakistan Brotherhood

There is now a formidable fresh basis for Pakistan's renewal of belligerence toward India over a sustained period. China's recent avowal of the deepest friendship for Islamabad goes well beyond the bland "all-weather friends" rubric we were familiar with.

The new metric of Beijing's political love of Islamabad's military- which, indeed, has defined the state of Pakistan for decades- is again best summed up by the People Republic's own official description of its proximity to Pakistan- that the friendship of the two is "higher than the mountains, deeper than the ocean, and sweeter than honey".

The Chinese are clever with this sort of propagandist word-play, but being a creative slogan of the Xi Jinping era, these are not mere words.

They are bolstered by China's Belt Road Initiative (BRI), whose centrepiece is the 60 billion dollar China-Pakistan Economic Corridor (CPEC), which links China to Pakistan's Gwadar port in coastal Baluchistan near the mouth of the Persian Gulf. Chinese power appears set on establishing a naval base here, astride the sea-lanes through which much of the world's oil trade passes.

CPEC's incalculable importance, and as a consequence Pakistan's value, in China's eyes, is best understood when it is seen that it is the brainchild of President Xi, who was placed on the same pedestal as Chairman Mao by the 19th Congress of the Communist Party of China last October.

The current leader's "Thoughts" have been sanctified in

the same manner as the legendary Mao Zedong's "Thoughts" were in an earlier era, and in the field of geopolitics the CPEC is the most eye-caching manifestation of Xi's strategic thinking and vision. It deals, above all, with the dynamics of radiating regional authority, and in constraining a long-term natural rival, India.

So, henceforth, it is no longer just Pakistan that New Delhi must deal with in reality, but the pair of Pakistan and China acting in tandem to confront Indian interests. That is why the Doklam standoff in the eastern Himalayas last summer had a deeper meaning for regional perceptions than we imagine.

The Pakistani terrorist leaders and groups whose credo is to attack India are now defended in world forums by China. We are also now directly face to face with China's politics and tactics in dealing with the Kashmir question since the CPEC passes through POK.

When in his first Tweet of 2018, US president Donald Trump hit out at Pakistan for its "lies and deceit" toward America after accepting 33 billion dollars in aid to fight terrorism, China publicly gave Islamabad cover, lauding its "sacrifices" in combating terrorism. This is a patently false construct, of course, as the Afghans and the Iranians will testify, not just the Indians.

It is precisely on account of the un-embarrassed and no holds barred emergence of the Sino-Pak compatibility quotient in the regional theatre—which makes Beijing give succour to South Asian terrorists, besides seeking to assume a large role in helping mind the Taliban along with Pakistan, a role that the Americans alone once appeared capable of—that India faces a very different Pakistan today than did Prime Ministers Vajpayee and Manmohan Singh.

Vajpayee could get Pervez Musharraf to give an undertaking in 2003 that Pakistani soil would not be permitted to be used by terrorists against India. This was because, being the kingpin behind Pakistan's botched Kargil incursion during Prime Minister Nawaz Sharief's tenure, Musharraf—when he became President on seizing power—had come under pressure from the Americans to mend fences with New Delhi. The US has always feared a possible nuclear confrontation between India and Pakistan if certain conventional military thresholds are crossed.

Washington under Trump still proclaims to harbour that anxiety. Islamabad tries to play on those fears in order to internationalise Kashmir. However, at the present juncture, on account of Islamabad's deepened Beijing links, Washington has ceded leverage in Islamabad.

Although its continuing long-term salience can hardly be in question, for now it is unlikely that Washington can persuade Islamabad to normalise ties with India through the simple expedient of reining in the terrorist brigades.

Besides anxieties relating to nukes, after Kargil President Clinton may have worried that the Indian Army might cross the LOC in retaliation and seize territory inside Pakistan to enhance its military leverage. He therefore urgently accepted PM Sharief's entreaty at the Blair House meeting in Washington to get the Vajpayee government to de-escalate.

Pakistani generals today, in contrast, have a very different play-book. They are all too conscious of Chinese munificence, and of an active Chinese counterweight that may shrink India's military leverage in relation to Islamabad. Doklam demonstrated this. In this scenario, the US could woo Pakistan in crucial ways to reduce Chinese influence.

Self-help is India's best bet. Step one must be to engender a favourable domestic political climate in Kashmir in order to neutralise a key Pakistani instrument.

The Modi government has been short-sighted on this. Step two is to enhance India's goodwill and political space in Afghanistan, which closes the circle in the context of Pakistan-inspired terrorism and the Pakistan army's revanchist aspirations.

Economic Times, January 21, 2018

Chabahar: The Port of Good Hope for Tehran, Kabul, New Delhi and More

The first shipment of wheat went through to Afghanistan using Iran's Chabahar port last month, and by early next year India would have shipped one million tons of the much-needed grain to the embattled country and build on its reservoir of goodwill there, which Islamabad has done hard to destroy in the last 15 years.

The Chabahar development demonstrates at one stroke that obstructionist Pakistan's veto stands removed in determining the tempo of our trade with Kabul.

Although this involves using land and sea to trade with land-locked Afghanistan, compared to the much shorter land corridor through Pakistan, the spinoffs of Chabahar port- if we can optimise these- confer advantages that cannot accrue using just the Pakistan route through Khyber Pass.

If projections hold, from the Indian perspective Chabahar should be fully operational by end-2018. That would mean the passage of cargo of a wider range, including engineering goods and electronics in the not too distant future.

The Chabahar avenue also allows the firming up of India's trade relations beyond Afghanistan to countries of Central Asia and on to St Petersburg in Russia, past the Caspian, by linking with what's called the North-South Transport Corridor, and the rail networks of Iran and more than a dozen other countries.

The travel time for goods all the way to Northern Europe from India via Chabahar is expected to be reduced by about half from the 45 days at present. The shortened time can permit the movement of certain categories of perishables to and from countries that are nearer on the route- Iran and Afghanistan.

The business profile can thus be altered for the benefit of all concerned. More than 2,000 trucks from Pakistan are said to pass Khyber on a daily basis, carrying everyday supplies to Afghanistan, all the way to Amu Dariya (the Oxus) in the north. Some of this trade, which is a factor for considerable Pakistani influence in Afghanistan, can be picked up by India when Chabahar opens up fully.

For the situation to sustain and allow the Chabahar channel to fulfil its promise as a geopolitical dividend for India, New Delhi will be required to put its head down and work for the long term- longer than the ten years visualised in the contract signed with Tehran in May last year, during the visit of Prime Minister Narendra Modi, to equip and run two multi-purpose cargo terminals.

Orders worth about 30 million dollars have now been placed by India for RMQC cranes. In all, equipment for the terminals at Chabahar being built by India is likely to cost about 85 million US dollars. India is also processing Iran's request for a credit of USD 150 million through the Exim Bank.

In addition, IRCON will have to brace itself to build the 640 kilometre railway link from Chabahar to Zahedan, from where Indian goods can connect to the Indian- built Zaranj-Delaram highway to convey goods to Afghanistan. The highway was built in 2011, after a lot of security nightmares, with the express purpose of carrying Indian exports and imports in relation to Afghanistan from Chabahar.

The Afghans may find, when the country's security situation settles down, that the sea-rail-road link constructed by India will be a positive factor for mineral extraction in northern Afghanistan and its evacuation.

Notwithstanding all the infrastructure works, the geopolitical meaning of Chabahar for India is ineluctably tied to the adequate appreciation of politics- bilateral, regional and international, and their deft and flexible management.

The Chinese and the Iranians have long played the game. The Russians have been at the centre of things since their super-power days and have strong stakes in Iran and Afghanistan. We too have to show we are ready to learn flexibility.

America, the world's pre-eminent power even in an international scenario approaching multi-polarity, is the elephant in the room. India's interest in developing the two small ports that make up the Chabahar complex dates back to 2003. But not much moved until 2015 when UN, European and some US sanctions on Iran were lifted following the signing of a nuclear agreement of the US-led world powers with Tehran.

The US under President Donald Trump is threatening to overturn this picture. Even so, in New Delhi recently, US secretary of state Rex Tillerson gave India relief with his statement that "genuine" business interests of countries with Iran will not be prejudiced on account of America.

At any rate, in the Iran-Afghanistan theatre, India will have to learn to manage its ties with Russia and China, given these countries' stakes here, even as it pursues close bonding with the US. The logic of a multi-polar world is that everyone does business with everyone else- may be America with North Korea too one day.

Economic Times, November 7, 2017

China's Doklam Gambit Misfires

It's evident that China's probing thrust in Doklam in June (principally it wasn't much more than that), more than anything else, was designed to test India's strategic antenna and its resolve to defend its self-image and status in the region and the world.

Beijing would have been surprised by the quickness of the Indian response, which demonstrated a readiness to not walk away from a "military standoff" if need be, while emphasising a diplomatic resolution, preferably one that is located in a benign political and philosophical perspective and framework which allows next-door neighbours that are leading powers with wide ambitions, to cooperate as a maxim but not flinch from competition.

This had been pretty much the story since Rajiv Gandhi and Deng Xiaoping reached a concord in 1988, followed up in 1993 by P.V. Narasimha Rao signing the border peace and tranquility agreement during his visit to China. This situation persisted through the Atal Behari Vajpayee years and the early Manmohan Singh years.

But China's ambitions skyrocketed with US companies locating operational bases in China on an impressive and unprecedented scale—very rapidly enriching its economy, industry and trade beyond the wildest dreams of the once aspiring communist state.

This permitted China to widen the gap in relation to the Indian economy- although India's GDP was ahead of China's in some years- and increase its military capabilities manifold. The "sweet spot" to underline the superiority of its geo-political influence over India was evidently now, Beijing reckoned, and not later, as ageing demographics are already corroding China's economy. Later may be late, and the show might not even take off, China seems to have also reckoned.

This is, fundamentally, the backdrop to Doklam. For Beijing, the point to disentangle, while planning Doklam was: how far could it go in pushing New Delhi with a view to belittling it before its smaller neighbours in South Asia, and also more widely among developing countries, specially in Africa, where both sides are trying to retain/spread influence through aid diplomacy?

It's plain to see the Chinese trick has misfired. Will Beijing still choose to go for even a limited military option?

Whether it does so or not, it has suddenly been confronted with uncertainty in ways it had not been while pushing the psychological frontier in the military field in the South China Sea in the past two years, when artificial atolls and islands were built up as naval and air stations in contemptuous disregard of the countries of the South China Sea littoral and of international legal opinion.

With the 19th Congress of the Chinese Communist Party only three months away, will President Xi Jinping, working to leave a mark on history, risk choosing uncertain and unintended outcomes in a high-profile contest with India? Time will tell. But pragmatists don't do that sort of thing.

Nevertheless, China remains zealous against India. The effort has moved to other spheres. After US President Donald Trump's recent policy announcement on Afghanistan, which asks Islamabad questions about its active help to terrorists and urges India to step up development assistance to Kabul, state councillor Yang Jiechi, who heads the core group making foreign policy in Beijing, said in a phone call to US secretary of state Rex Tillerson that Islamabad's "sovereignty and reasonable security concerns" in Afghanistan needed to be met.

There couldn't be a more succinct endorsement of the silly Pakistani narrative that India's benign presence in Afghanistan (which Kabul has consistently given high marks to) threatens Pakistan's security; ergo India should leave Afghanistan.

Never before has Beijing promoted Pakistan's case in respect of Afghanistan with such monumental irrationality and brazenness. This "coming out" has coincided with Pakistan lately agreeing to serve as a semi-colony of China—providing it land through Indian territory in PoK to reach Gwadar in Balochistan on the Arabian sea where a Chinese naval harbour is to be built, and also batting enthusiastically for Beijing's OBOR initiative.

OBOR is a clear geopolitical move to undercut Indian influence or its potential in South Asia and in the Western Indian Ocean region touching the eastern shores of Africa. But its most conspicuous and immediate evidence is seen to the northwest of India. Evidently, the game is that it will now be China and Pakistan together in Afghanistan, seeking to edge India out. This had been in the works since US President Barack Obama decided to draw down troops from Afghanistan, retaining only a residual force there.

It is to be seen how China will recalibrate with President Trump shifting the terms of US engagement in the AfPak region. Much would also depend on how India imagines its own future role in the Afghan theatre. Any slackening, among other things, is apt to give China a sense of fulfilment and make it push harder against India strategically on a wider canvas.

The effort to curb India by using the Pakistan proxy of course began a long time ago. In the recent period, it was given shape with China trying to block the India-US civil nuclear agreement through surreptitious diplomacy. When this didn't work, the game moved to trying to keep India out of the Nuclear Suppliers Group. This was done explicitly. Crassly, the Chinese also kept blocking Indian (and later US) moves in the UN to punish the Pakistani terrorist group Jaish-e-Mohammed and its leader Masood Azhar.

Apart from the Pakistan-Afghan region to our west, which Beijing is hoping to render inhospitable terrain for New Delhi, it is also doing what it can to use its considerable economic muscle to bulldoze Nepal to our east in adopting postures inimical to India. A similar effort is on in Sri Lanka. It is, of course, up to India how to dispel these moves through diplomacy, politics, and permissible use of available military leverage.

Let's cut to 1962. V.K. Krishna Menon was acute when he told Michael Brecher that the real reason for the Chinese attack was the desire to teach India a lesson.

Jawaharlal Nehru was a giant on the world stage. India was poor but was internationally sought after in the political realm. China felt impelled to give it a thwack to whittle Nehru's—and India's—prestige in the world to enhance its own standing.

A similar mindset is at work now. The difference is that churlishness and desperation is making Beijing sound like North Korea these days. If India stays the course in Doklam and Afghanistan, the dynamics in the South China Sea could change.

Asian Age & The Deccan Chronicle, August 29, 2017

The Chinese Way or the Highway

The Chinese are playing their One Belt One Road (OBOR) move, a massive once-in-a-lifetime geopolitical lunge in multiple domains, as a benign attempt at infrastructure-building and economic connectivity. For all practical purposes Beijing has criticised India for keeping away from OBOR which, it says, will be a significant factor for stability and meta-regional development, and therefore peace and prosperity.

This is a bit rich. Since when did Beijing care for infrastructure and regional connectivity unless it was in the driver's seat? It is evident that China is upset with India for calling a spade a spade and making it clear that it wasn't ready to bless its strategic quests.

For those who are not blind, Afghanistan to Dhaka would have been a seamless journey for road traffic by now—in the process transforming lives through billions of dollars of trade and investments—if Pakistan had not played mischief and prevented the flow of goods from Bangladesh and India through its territory into Afghanistan.

Kabul's and New Delhi's pleadings fell on deaf ears in Islamabad. It is hard to recall a single instance when the politburo in Beijing urged its all-weather friends, Pakistan's top-shots in olive green, to think of connectivity, stability and development and letting Afghanistan prosper by trading as far afield as Bangladesh.

We should go back further. Pakistan placed roadblocks in every SAARC forum dedicated to the expansion of trade, investments and connectivity within the grouping. China, which at one stage desired to participate in SAARC, did not see it fit to advise the generals in Rawalpindi to reflect on the virtuous cycle that would be generated if their "nyet" mentality was forsaken in the context of SAARC connectivity.

It can be argued that what China, along with Pakistan, want to see most dearly is the closing down of SAARC and the luring of SAARC members into the OBOR network. In that way they envisage the loosening of India's commercial, financial, infrastructure and economic linkages with the sub-continent (minus Pakistan). This will be an impossibility, of course.

Among most SAARC countries, it is not just capital and finance that move, but also labour and culture, and there are no inimical distances and harsh terrains to traverse, as in the OBOR case, against which Jia Qingguo, a Beijing university scholar and member of the Study Committee of the People's Political Consult-ative Conference, had cautioned. And much of the labour force moves to take advantage of the markets in India.

Jia had worried about the "wishful thinking" aspect of OBOR, which (in its maritime as well as land *avatars*) would touch the eastern regions of Africa, besides the Maldives, Sri Lanka, Nepal, Bangladesh, Myanmar and the wholly unpredictable regions of Central and West Asia, to say nothing of the territories from the Karakoram to Balochistan in Pakistan that are ripe with upheavals of many kinds and degrees.

But Beijing still thinks the iron is hot, although some of its lead thinkers on geopolitical affairs worry. Xi Jinping is lord and master and his word is law as he is already sitting in the pantheon which has only two other occupants, Mao and Deng Xiaoping. In his lifetime Xi hopes to transcend beyond mere economic influence to seek to radiate extensive geopolitical power.

In this effort China's investible surpluses are indispensable. These can't travel eastward. South Korea and Japan can do without Chinese infrastructure support. Therefore, it is desperate to go westward, a much poorer part of the world for a long stretch.

The real focus, in the foreseeable future is, of course, Pakistan, which is China's gateway to Gwadar port on the Makran coast and the Arabian Sea, where a major naval facility to harbour nuclear-powered submarines is envisioned as another useful check on India. The vehicle for this is the China-Pakistan Economic Corridor (CPEC) on which the Pakistanis placed a value of $46 billion (over an undefined period).

In the event, Beijing has little choice, but to ride roughshod on India's sovereignty concerns in PoK. People's Liberation Army (PLA) West Zone troops moved into PoK in the guise of workers on infrastructure projects some time ago- not only in Gilgit-Baltistan, but also in the Jhelum and Neelum River valleys, just across from Baramullah on the Indian side. (It is not unlikely that a Chinese trooper might be hit if the Indian Army shells with medium artillery in that area!)

Since early 2015, when Xi Jinping, first made a reference to CPEC and OBOR on a visit to Pakistan, colonies of Chinese labourers and supervisors, PLA's sappers and miners in effect, have proliferated. They are already thought to be a division-strong, although it is hard to be certain about figures.

The Indians raised red flags in 2009-10. The point made was that a Chinese road cannot be built through Indian territory (even if it is under Pakistan's occupation). In Gilgit-Baltistan, the Asian Development Bank had declined to finance power projects unless a no-objection certificate was obtained from India, but the "social imperialists" sitting in Beijing have had no qualms about the same projects. Spreading strategic influence has trumped theory and morality.

On this and related issues, India has practically been silent on the diplomatic front since Xi's 2015 visit to Pakistan, the effective date for announcing OBOR to the world. It is extraordinary that New Delhi kept its thoughts to itself until the very last minute even on the issue of attending the two-day Belt Road Forum conclave in Beijing last Sunday and Monday. This is the lowest ebb that pusillanimity can reach.

New Delhi should have been out campaigning long before that—telling all concerned that the social imperialists were trying to spread their wings, and that eventually not much was likely to accrue to the smaller nations that look to be taken in. Look at the example of Sri Lanka, they might have been told, where every dollar supposedly invested as soft loan by China was taken out with neat profit. India evidently has some way to go in its geopolitical positioning.

Asian Age & The Deccan Chronicle, May 21, 2017

For PM and BJP, a Reality Check

At the BJP national meet at Kozhikode, Kerala, on Saturday, Prime Minister Narendra Modi broke a weeklong spell of ward-rumming that had broken out after the Uri terrorist attack. Leading the band were BJP leaders. They were merely being who they are—the natural representatives of the party's rank and file who have been weaned on the idea of sounding "strong" and "raining blows" on perceived foes, especially Pakistan, on account of the religious dimension.

Bowing to their ideological compulsions, and following in the footsteps of the RSS and BJP leaders (Modi himself is a good example of this when he was Gujarat chief minister, and later as he campaigned in the 2014 Lok Sabha elections), these cadres look for simple—even simplistic—solutions to complex problems, such as ties with Pakistan.

In the RSS-BJP lore, a heave and a blow is all it takes. We may recall that after the nuclear weapons test when Atal Behari Vajpayee was Prime Minister, a leading light of the BJP establishment in Delhi who had been a cabinet minister, a fine but simple man, had invited Pakistan to a wrestle.

In an unwarranted show of belligerence he struck his thighs with his open palms in the North Indian manner to denote posing a challenge by the obviously superior side. When the news of the testing of the Pakistani nukes came days after, there was understandable silence. So, that's who they are.

Television too was dutifully obliging. Screens were filled with silly "debates" in which a nearly undifferentiated school of experts—chosen from the cadre of retired diplomats, former security bureaucrats, and ex-military folk who abound in Delhi—expanded on "strike options". Thank God these guys exist, or our television will have to invent them to keep going.

At Kozhikode, the Prime Minister busted the narrative of the merry war-gamers. He showed a remarkable sense of realism and fell in line with what's come to be known as "strategic restraint", displayed by all his predecessors except Indira Gandhi in 1971.

Mr. Vajpayee showed it in 2001 when Parliament was attacked, and Manmohan Singh in 2008 after the attack on Mumbai. Both ran coalition governments. But Modi runs a government in which his party has more than a comfortable majority.

That's the lesson. While war cannot be forsworn by any State as a matter of principle, in dealing with Pakistan it cannot come as an easy, obvious and only option to India whether a leader in Parliament heads a motley coalition or a triumphalist majority of "Hindu nationalists", the expression Modi favoured for himself in an interview two years ago.

This is for two principal reasons. Prosecuting even a short war (a country like Pakistan, even if it were foolhardy enough to use battlefield nuclear weapons against India, is unlikely to last a week) will extract sharp economic costs and push down our economic advance as a nation in the medium term.

Two, the external environment is not likely to accept an outbreak of hostilities for a variety of reasons, but essentially because the principal powers, especially China, the US, and Saudi Arabia, are unlikely to want another possible India-Pakistan conflict at the present juncture.

Asian Age & The Deccan Chronicle, September 26, 2016

Nuclear Suppliers Group Membership: Don't get Chinese Checkered

The manner in which the government has pushed India's case for membership of the Nuclear Suppliers Group (NSG), the informal cartel of 48 countries that regulates international commerce in nuclear materials and technologies, defies the diplomatic law of gravity.

China openly helps build Pakistan as a nuclear state, although our western neighbour had shocked the world by its act of nuclear black-marketing, and was caught. Nevertheless, in all likelihood, it is under Chinese encouragement that Islamabad applied for NSG membership a week after the Indian application was made.

Let's try and guess why Beijing might be so keen. To secure Pakistan a place at the table where international rules of nuclear trade are framed when all Islamabad has done is to wilfully break those rules? NSG membership is granted by consensus among its members. Given Islamabad's record, how many countries are likely to veer round to forming a consensus around Pakistan?

In the event, it is a no- brainer that the Pakistani application was made so that Beijing may, sounding all very holy, talk about rules and procedures in the matter of the Indian application, and have it overlooked.

China's logic runs as follows: India has not signed the nuclear non-proliferation treaty (NPT) and NSG membership so far has been open to NPT signatories only. No exceptions should be made for any one country. (India seeks to get over this by presenting its shiny non-proliferation record but China does not hear, though most NSG members- including the US and Canada among major nuclear materials suppliers- do.)

China does not directly state the converse it has in mind- that Pakistan, which has also not signed the NPT, too should be made a NSG member if India is. It merely says that if non-signatories to the NPT are to become members, then the present general body should reach a consensus on this.

And how does India read this? That China is not against India's membership of the NSG—to quote from external affairs minister Sushma Swaraj's press conference last Sunday, with foreign secretary S. Jaishankar by her side (which signals the PMO's endorsement of the line)—but seems to have some difficulties relating to "procedures", though we still expect that Beijing would be brought around by June 24 when the NSG plenary is slated to meet in Seoul.

Is this naive or surreal? Right after Swaraj spoke, Beijing declared that the Indian application was not on the Seoul agenda.

The strangest things do happen. Jashankar had secretly flown to Beijing last week to woo China. His talks there were meant to ready the ground for a possible meeting between Prime Minister Narendra Modi and China's President Xi Jinping in Tashkent on June 23 on the sidelines of the Shanghai Cooperation Organisation, a day before NSG's Seoul plenary. May be, the political bigwigs do the unexpected in a fit of the deepest camaraderie.

But wait. What's the price India will have to be pay? Xi is a tough nut. After Modi's huge 2014 victory, the Chinese leader visited India and sat on a swing with the Indian PM on the banks of the Sabarmati, and just then his soldiers created a military incident in Ladakh and our troops went eye-ball to eye-ball for days together. Xi did not bat an eyelid. So, that's who he is. What's the price he would demand for a little help with the NSG matter?

We don't know. But the external affairs minister hinted

on Sunday that India doesn't mind if Pakistan also joined the NSG. News reports suggest that Jaishankar canvassed the line when he met his Chinese counterpart recently.

If this is true, and India publicly agrees to show brotherhood to Pakistan on the nuclear question when the reason for the existence of Islamabad's bomb is its perceived enmity with India (and no other—as is evident from its nuclear doctrine), it will be a travesty—a diplomatic foray without a shred of principle. Pakistan still won't get its NSG membership. No one other than China would endorse it, and even China won't have to as it would never come to that. But India would have made itself a laughing stock among civilised nations.

What's the urgency about India being made a NSG member on June 24? None whatsoever. Thanks to US support, back in 2008 India obtained a clean waiver from the NSG and is already entitled to purchase nuclear wares internationally.

Economic Times, July 22, 2016

A Zero for Modi on Diplomacy

The past ten days have cruelly exposed the foreign policy pretensions of the Modi government as deep embarrassment has simultaneously been caused to India from three crucial quarters: Pakistan and China in our immediate neighbourhood operating in tandem, and internationally the United States.

With the US, Prime Minister Narendra Modi has sought to develop a "global partnership"—going beyond the mere "strategic partnership" of an earlier time—since President Barack Obama arrived in New Delhi as our chief guest for Republic Day last year.

The so-called "global partnership" regime might be usefully seen as the base camp to reaching the Mount Everest of being America's "strategic ally", or at least a "non-Nato strategic ally". That honour has thus far been showered on countries like Egypt and Pakistan, the two biggest recipients of US military hardware, which are also military dictatorships in effect.

The direction in which Modi wishes to travel to elevate India's status in the world is thus clear. We must, of course, ask ourselves if the status of a "leading power", let alone a "global power" or "great power" such as the US, China or the European Union, is achievable for a country mired in disquieting poverty for close to one half of its population, and burdened with a savings deficit to fuel the greatly enhanced investments required to maintain a place on the high growth path.

At the same time, India is having to endure on a sustained

basis a worsening social climate on account of religious neo-imperialism being sought to be pushed by the Hindutva brigade indulged by the regime. Domestic peace and harmony, it can't be emphasised enough, is as great a requirement for achieving prominence and weight in the international system as accretion to economic wealth and development of military might for purposes of power projection.

In any case, strategies being pursued by this government to raise India's position in the world—by dovetailing our strategic and security preferences to the overarching US "vision", especially for the Indo-Pacific region,—have not been brought to the forum of Parliament for discussion, although it is possible that they have been gone over in the counsels of the RSS and the Sangh Parivar, of which the ruling BJP is an element.

The irony is worth noting that for many decades our neighbour Pakistan has also sought to derive its strategic solace by linking up with American dreams through the period of the Cold War in its effort to militarise rapidly and shore up its domestic economy. That trajectory has been widened for some years to attract the munificence of across-the-board Chinese assistance, as befits the description of "all-weather friendship" between Beijing and Islamabad.

Thus, Pakistan finds itself today in the coveted position of being cosseted by two permanent members of the UN Security Council who fulfil its military needs and its infrastructural requirements, and give it invaluable political manoeuvre room.

At the cost of causing deep resentment in India, Washington recently cleared the supply of a fresh batch of F-16 fighter aircraft and attack helicopters to Islamabad, although it knows that historically Pakistani generals have aimed US-supplied military equipment at India.

Even as the Obama administration decided to go ahead with sending high-value military goods to Pakistan that will doubtless be used against this country, at his press conference after the Nuclear Security summit in Washington at the end of last month, which Mr Modi—for unfathomable reasons—attended with the air of a prancing bridegroom, Mr Obama berated both India and Pakistan, as if spanking two naughty boys together, for maintaining large nuclear arsenals while having military doctrines that were "continually headed in the wrong direction".

The US leader disregarded India's nuclear rectitude. He forgave Pakistan for acquiring its bomb-making capability on the clandestine nuclear supermarket. He stopped short of highlighting the danger of terrorists stealing from the Pakistani nuclear arsenal although this is a cause of openly voiced worry.

The truth is that indirectly, and very consequentially, Obama was hitting out at India's military doctrine of Cold Start, whose very mention frustrates and angers Pakistan, and provides the military generals in Islamabad a much-needed political ballast. Cold Start postulates that Indian forces will rapidly make a retaliatory conventional warfare move inside Pakistan and hold territory as a hedge against a likely Pakistani nuclear strike since Islamabad revels in its nuclear doctrine which underscores its nuclear "first strike" posture against India.

The government's reaction in New Delhi to Obama's officious pseudo-moral posturing was far from angry. The Modi government was content to note that Obama had shown a lack of understanding of the Indian military doctrine. Such a cavalier disregard of our crucial security concerns is hard to imagine. India has not before been known for a tail-between-the-legs attitude towards a great power.

It is in this background of extreme American solicitousness that Pakistan has just delivered India a diplomatic black eye. After India received a Pakistani technical team, which included a senior ISI officer, to investigate the Pathankot terrorist attack, and requested a reciprocal visit to Pakistan by Indian investigators to interrogate Jaish-e-Mohammed leaders, including its notorious chief Masood Azhar, the Pakistani high commissioner in New Delhi announced that for now the talks between the two countries stood "suspended".

In this period, when India tried to get Masood Azhar named in the UN list as an "international terrorist"—so that his movements and financial transactions could be tracked with a view to preventing future terrorist acts—China conspicuously stepped in to block the effort, thus proclaiming to the world its tight security embrace of Pakistan.

Since Modi assumed office two years ago, much of his government's diplomatic energy has been expended on making high-profile forays into enhancing the spirit of ties with Washington, Islamabad and Beijing in a highly personalised manner, with contempt for institutional knowledge and experience.

This was being hailed as foreign and security policy alacrity by the RSS, BJP and the favoured bureaucrats of the top-tier, who have pointedly contrasted what they see as present-day innovativeness and dynamism with the diplomatic languidness of the Manmohan Singh years.

After the triple rebuff of recent days, one truly wonders, though. The much maligned Dr Singh was at no stage in his ten years in office humiliated by Washington, Islamabad and Beijing in quick order within a space of less than 10 days. Is it Modi who is being strong-armed, or is it India?

Asian Age & The Deccan Chronicle, April 11, 2016

PM's Walk in the Woods with Pak

Since the Pakistani state is military-dominated and military-controlled, it needs an adversarial cause for its existential justification, and this is easily found in democratic India which also happens to be a "Hindu state" as far as the military's perception goes, since Pakistan's military regards itself as a keeper of the flame, an embodiment of the notion of the "ghazi" confronting unbelievers. There is enough scholarly writing which underlines this.

After Pathankot, which is now so clear the government severely mismanaged, Prime Minister Narendra Modi seems to be staying the course on a diplomatic opening with Pakistan, fervently hoping that a modicum of success will help eclipse the memory of the attack and the Indian mishandling of it, and neutralise domestic criticism.

It is evident though that the persistence with so-called diplomacy is in return for nothing. It seems more a personal prestige thing since the Prime Minister himself had led the opening hand—personalised diplomacy at its very worst, in keeping with Modi's reputation for "event management".

If Islamabad—or more precisely Rawalpindi, Pakistan's army headquarters—were serious in giving diplomacy a helping hand, it would not wait for mathematical proof in nabbing those responsible for the Pathankot strike, as it had done in the case of 26/11. It would, instead, take the military courts route as it did in the case of the militants who had attacked a school in Peshawar killing children, and sent the criminals to the gallows in double quick time.

Our armed forces are not amused with the handling of the Pathankot affair, which seems to have put the National Security Guard at odds with the army, thanks to some boyscout imaginings in the office of the national security adviser, who directly reports to the Prime Minister.

Pushing the diplomatic envelop at this stage doesn't seem to make sense to many seasoned hands in Indian diplomacy and the security establishment, to say nothing of the lay public.

Friendship with Pakistan is a laudable project. In general, diplomacy with a perceived adversary is perhaps even more necessary than with a friend, at least to ensure that neither side flies off-course and creates a regrettable situation. But Modi has too few cards in his hand at the moment, whatever his reasons for taking two steps forward in dealing with Pakistan.

Especially after a terrible incident like Pathankot, on Pakistan's part there should be good reason to show empathy with India if Islamabad means business, more so if the victim country is not appearing to be aggressive, and is appealing to the good sense of the other side so that talks may continue. But there are few signs of Pakistani reasonableness on view, other than the optics. Which means India is being taken for a ride and not just its Prime Minister, who champions personalised diplomacy.

With the Lahore "stopover" it is birthday diplomacy these days, earlier there was "sari diplomacy" (with our Prime Minister sending saris for Mr Sharif's mother as a token of sincerity), and in between "diplomacy on the swings" (with Chinese leader Xi Jinping in Ahmedabad even as his country's troops forced their way into the Indian side of the perceived boundary). While Modi presses ahead looking for a viable diplomatic opening, Islamabad has made it plain that the mobile phone numbers dialled by the terrorists from Pathankot—which India confidently forwarded to the Pakistani authorities as "evidence"—are not even registered in Pakistan.

Simply put, Islamabad is saying the patrons of the attack

are not from Pakistan. If that's the case, there's not much left to say. Let's just recall that when India had similarly presented phone numbers and call intercepts as "evidence" after the Mumbai attacks, the Pakistan foreign secretary visiting New Delhi for talks derisively described the material submitted by India as "literature", not evidence. In effect, the same Shakespearean tragedy is now being replayed, but the tenor is softer. That's the only difference.

When Prime Minister Atal Behari Vajpayee had asked Pakistan to hand over Dawood Ibrahim, Islamabad switched off its earplugs. All Vajpayee got in return was the attack on the Indian Parliament. When Prime Minister Manmohan Singh asked for the guilty in the Mumbai attacks to be tried with sincerity in Pakistan, and asked for the voice samples of Zakiur Rehman Lakhvi, the operations chief for the 26/11 attacks, he met with a cold rebuff, although Pakistan kept urging him to visit it as a mark of goodwill.

Now it is Prime Minister Modi's turn to be beguiled. Thus, there is the mystery of the supposed arrest of Maulana Masood Azhar, the chief of Jaish-e-Mohammed, the Inter-Services Intelligence-nurtured specifically anti-India terrorist outfit that had mounted the Parliament attack and seems to be behind Pathankot.

This is being officially interpreted in India as the Pakistan government being reasonable; worse, that it is bowing to Indian pressure, if some of the purple prose in Indian news reporting at the behest of unnamed official sources is to be believed. So much is being made in India of Azhar's "preventive detention" or "arrest" that we completely forget that the same man had been arrested for a whole year after the attack on the Indian Parliament in 2001. But he was never charged and was let off on court orders.

In any case, the Jaish is technically a proscribed organisation already. So, why the big song and dance if its chief is picked up for questioning (in order to keep up diplomatic appearances with India)? Propaganda overkill can rebound when the truth comes out, as Modi will learn. The American public had been led to believe—thanks to a pliable media—that the US was winning the war in Vietnam. When 50,000 body bags came home and defeat could no longer be hidden, public psychology in the US turned numb and was utterly disoriented.

Modi seems to have learnt little from the parliament attack, Kargil, the Mumbai attacks, or for that matter Pathankot, which happened on his watch.He might as well come out and say that from the Indian side terrorism is no more going to be a component of the composite or comprehensive dialogue process with Pakistan. That is the direction in which he appears to be moving.

Asian Age & The Deccan Chronicle, January 17, 2016

Pak: India Takes a Myopic View

Nations need diplomacy, or they'll be readying for war all the time; Prime Minister Narendra Modi needs megaphone diplomacy. Very few things have gone right as a result.

The Prime Minister has been practising his particular trade from the day he was sworn in. It won him not a little applause. His name rang out from Madison Square Gardens in New York to Sydney Harbour. In those places, and a few others, his name will perhaps continue to re-echo so long as the Modi government softens up India's domestic market for foreign capital, trade and investment thrusts. But the neighbourhood has turned out a different story, especially Pakistan.

Not much has gone right, in spite of flashes of optimism early on that turned out to be false, with shock results emanating from Beijing and Islamabad, our largest and difficult neighbours, in response to the kindest overtures from Modi's diplomatic repertoire.

China was much advertised. Modi was its darling since he had been visiting the neighbour to the north from the time he was chief minister. But when President Xi Jinping arrived in Ahmedabad to sway on the same swing in the park as the Prime Minister, his heavy-duty troops showed up with him.

Men of the People's Liberation Army swarmed into what we thought was our side of the unclear boundary and just stayed put. After weeks of cajoling, they did vacate, but not before taking a toll on India-China ties. With Pakistan, sari diplomacy—despatch of that elegant Indian ladies' apparel for Pakistan Prime Minister Nawaz Sharif's mother—was the Indian leader's chosen instrument to create a favourable environment for beneficial bilateralism.

By now, however, in a space of just over a year, the early expectation of goodwill on both sides has evaporated, replaced by a discourse of threats. Foolishly Pakistan's national security adviser Sartaj Aziz has sought to let India know that his country possesses nuclear weapons.

Such an essay at brinkmanship, it should perhaps be said, has its roots in India's failure to gauge that the regional dynamics have taken a new turn of late—that recent events have given Islamabad the confidence to think that a new phase in India-Pakistan relations has been struck, and that this is to its advantage. New Delhi simply failed to read the wind and continued to treat India-Pakistan relations in the business-as-usual fashion.

Two parallel frameworks have helped set the stage for a new turn in India-Pakistan relations, and India will need a wholly different toolkit to negotiate this unexpected bend in the road. Perhaps there is insufficient awareness of this even now in New Delhi, and until we re-gain our bearings there is not much likelihood of striking an effective course.

The first is the field of post-US Afghanistan. America and China, in their respective self-interest, have decreed that Pakistan be given a free hand in shaping events in Afghanistan in the foreseeable future, with Washington and Beijing playing god-fairy. The departing US special representative for Afghanistan and Pakistan, Dan Feldman, informed an American audience not long ago that long-term stability in Afghanistan would be elusive without Pakistan's support.

This means the US takes it as an obligation to lay the gifts it possesses before Pakistan in the expectation that the Pakistan army will be able to extract appropriate behaviour from the Taliban who have been sheltering in Pakistan since America threw them out of Kabul in 2001. The Pakistan army naturally has its tail up.

The process of official negotiations between the Islamabad-controlled Taliban and the Ashraf Ghani government in Kabul is now underway in Pakistan, not in Afghanistan or a third cou`ntry. Whatever President Ghani's own pre-disposition, he believes that for his own good he must do as America and China say.

This explains his government's less than solicitous treatment of India of late. China has turned out a proximate ally of Washington in this. It has underwritten Pakistan for decades and believes that if it can be of assistance in reinstalling the Taliban in power in Kabul with Islamabad's political and social support, it will be able to checkmate its own terrorism and extremism problem in Uighur country in Xinjiang, which abuts Afghanistan.

Besides, China hopes to be in position to extract Afghanistan's considerable mineral resource. In the event of the new equation maturing to China's and Pakistan's satisfaction, India could be faced with a new Great Wall of China in its entry into the Central Asian theatre, which has a natural and easy passage through Afghanistan.

If the Pakistan army has been buoyed by the US and Chinese interests coinciding in Pakistan's favour in the Afghan theatre, the recent Chinese assurance of an infrastructure investment of nearly $50 billion through the socalled One Belt, One Road mechanism inside Pakistan—incidentally, a good deal of it inside the territories of Kashmir under Pakistani occupation—has lifted the Pakistani capitalist class and its political establishment, to say nothing of the Army.

Together, the pattern of twin developments has given the Pakistani ruling establishment a leg-up of the kind that has not been seen before, including when Pakistan had entered Central Treaty Organisation (CENTO) as a check on communism (and India) decades ago under American tutelage and guardianship, and created a wholly new paradigm in South Asian affairs.

In this new heady atmosphere for Pakistan, the basic *sutra* of bilateralism in settling disputes with India, thrown up by the Simla Agreement and the Lahore Declaration, may be treated as being as good as dead.

If the planned meeting of the national security advisers of the two countries did not take place on account of the freshly-fuelled Pakistani irredentism owing to a Sino-US tango working in Islamabad's favour, it is best to accept the reality that the meeting was doomed from the start—that it was dead on the water.

In New Delhi, an appreciation of a new turn being formed in the road—the setting of a new stage in India-Pakistan ties-failed to materialise because the institutional discipline of diplomacy received short shrift in government as a maladroit Prime Minister's Office took charge, taking itself to be the centre of the universe.

Asian Age & The Deccan Chronicle, August 31, 2015

End SAARC Pessimism

As Prime Minister Narendra Modi embarks on a trip infused with the neighbourhood spirit this week to attend the 18th Saarc summit in Kathmandu, he may reflect on a certain irony—that while the Indian subcontinent was one of the economically most active regions of the world (Britain's Indian possession being the "jewel in the crown" of the empire over which the sun never set) despite the fact that its GDP remained somewhat stagnant in the last four decades of colonial rule, the collection of countries of the South Asia region is economically among the most sluggish in our own day.

What was not much over half-a-century ago practically a common market in geo-economic terms (of course it was the same country), Saarc is today the world's least integrated trade and economic bloc, although tariffs have been coming down steadily since 2006 when South Asia Free Trade Agreement (SAFTA) became a reality.

The broad idea is to have tariffs lowered to five per cent or less from their current rates. That will help, but further tariff reduction alone is not likely to appreciably push exports and imports among the eight member countries of the grouping.

Much more challenging impediments—that frequently arise as a function of politics in specific cases- need to be overcome in order to get ahead. Remember, the official intra-Saarc trade is only around six per cent of the overall international trade of the Saarc countries. This rises to a mere 10 per cent if the unofficial trade is taken into account.

The so-called sensitive list of items that each country arms itself with in the (usually) vain hope that such a strategm might help nurse and protect particular sub-sectors of its economy must be drastically pruned if not scrapped for trade within Saarc to move up.

Even with the crippling handicap of non-tariff barriers (NTBs) that are monumentally present within Saarc as an inhibiting agent, India-Pakistan trade, for instance, can grow significantly if only the negative list were consciously emaciated. This could have an electrifying effect on the entire Saarc system since the relations between these two countries are seen as an obstacle to Saarc's growth.

Another trade-killing factor within Saarc, without which no discussion in relation to the grouping can be meaningful, is the non-tariff barrier or non-tariff measures. Trade economists inform us that if this obstacle were removed or minimised, the trade-enhancing effect will be greater than if tariffs were brought to near-zero.

NTBs can take many forms. Their net effect is to increase the cost of trade, dispirit the trader, and not permit consumers of a particular country of a regional grouping to get the best price for a commodity from another country within that region.

Red tape, irksome customs procedures, trucks waiting for a fortnight at the international border between countries, unreasonable sanitary and phyto-sanitary standards—meaning all the various reasons that the goods of one country may not become available to citizens of another even when tariffs are not the issue—are typical NTBs. They are dynamite for intra-Saarc trade.

When we speak of British India having been an active economic player, and goods moving across the subcontinent with ease, it is a fair assumption that the absence of negative lists and NTBs (much of the region was one country) would have been a trade-promoting factor in that era. Not having this cushion is a setback in our times and efforts need to be stepped up to remove the undesirable elements of the trading ecosystem.

But we need to work toward anther leap as well. Since what is now Saarc was virtually one country in the colonial period, there was no impediment to movement of either capital or labour across the vast terrain. Hindu merchant bankers from the upper Sindh and southern Punjab belt (in colonial India) lent money all the way to Kabul and sometimes went as far north as Merv, across the Oxus. It was the same currency all the way through as the Indian rupee of the day was legal tender as far afield as Aden.

With equal felicity, certain specialised branches of Pashtun or Pathan traders, who were Muslims from the Afghan area, went with their wares all the way to Bengal (both East and West). The story of one such Pathan yielded Kabuliwallah, Rabindranath Tagore's famous short story which was captured as a popular motion picture.

There was "trans-border connectivity" in those blessed times when roads didn't exist. This writer has had the good fortune of speaking with traders in the bazaars of Kandahar not long ago who spoke of family memory of grand-uncles and grandfathers who had trading establishments in Bombay and beyond, and bemoan the Partition of India that ended a way of life.

We can't bring back those times. There can't even be a customs union as that would mean aligning tariffs along eight countries, many of whom are mired in mutual political mistrust. There cannot be a South Asia Community like the European Community, for a common currency is impossible to think of for now. But we can certainly think of "SAFTA plus" by thinking of cross-border linkages and connectivity, especially in the areas of transport and energy.

It is time Saarc pessimism gave way to a more positive spirit that induces action in the post-SAFTA phase. The time of cross-border connectivity and energy and transport corridors may have arrived. These will be development corridors really.

All countries and regions which lie in their path will benefit from the economic bustle and buzz they are intended to create. This is the message Modi is expected to unveil in Kathmandu.

At the 7th South Asia Economic Summit preceding the Saarc summit, prepared by Research and Information Systems (RIS) in New Delhi earlier this month, a leading Bangladesh Saarc veteran reminded the audience that the spectacular economic rise of China had caused the rise of its smaller neighbours as well, but this was not true of the sustained lift in India's growth trajectory over a 15-year stretch.

This seems a fair point. The lacuna in India's case is the absence of financial and infrastructural linkages with neighbours. The survival of Saarc these 30 years is itself a testimony to its need.

Asian Age & The Deccan Chronicle, November 24, 2014

The Chinese Tango

In the history of India's dealings with the world, there have been few moments more humiliating than the planned and unblinking encroachment by Chinese soldiers of our ground on the (admittedly undefined) boundary in Ladakh—and then staying put there in a show of orchestrated truculence—when President Xi Jinping was on a state visit here and was being feted by Prime Minister Narendra Modi, first in Ahmedabad and later in the national capital.

Not exactly known for delicacy in these matters, the Chinese on this occasion did one better than when they had invaded Vietnam, a "brother" socialist country, when Atal Behari Vajpayee, India's external affairs minister at the time, was on Chinese soil. They simply went ahead and invaded Indian territory when their supreme leader was on Indian soil.

If anything, this is the high-altitude equivalent of gunboat diplomacy—the show of diplomacy when, in fact, the threat of use of superior fire power is being indicated—which was made an art form by colonial expansionists and has been improved upon since by their modern-day cousins of all shades.

Beijing won't cut much ice if it sought to argue that since the boundary is not demarcated, soldiers on both sides stray into each other's area unknowingly. This is true enough, but what the People's Liberation Army (PLA) boys engaged in was an open-eyed intrusive measure with an unconcealed purpose.

They were single-minded. They were not straying. They

worked to a plan. And they received political orders from the top. In such matters things don't work any other way in the People's Republic. The Manmohan Singh government had nearly met the same fate last year.

When Chinese Premier Li Keqiang was about to arrive in India, PLA troops thrust into the Indian side and occupied ground. The Prime Minister rushed his external affairs minister Salman Khurshid to Beijing as PLA and Indian soldiers stood "eyeball to eyeball", hinting that the Chinese leader's impending visit could be imperilled if the unpleasant situation of China's making persisted.

This worked wonders. The PLA contingents backed off. Beijing apprehended ignominy and shame if a scheduled visit of its Prime Minster was called off. Li, it may be recalled, was mint- new at his post then and had virtually cadged an invitation from Prime Minister Manmohan Singh when the two were in Africa. And yet, the Chinese mandarins thought nothing of planning a show of force as their premier was to touch down in India to talk trade, investments, and a strategic dimension to the relationship in the interest of peace and stability in the region and in the heavens, and more of such blather.

Historical insight suggests that none of this is meant, and that we should tread warily in dealing with the Chinese and managing our relationship with them. The pattern of boundary talks with China since 1993 when Prime Minister P.V. Narasimha Rao travelled to Beijing and signed an agreement to keep the Line of Control or LAC "tranquil"—free of small and big incidents involving the military until a formal boundary is negotiated—is revealing.

The foremost lesson here is that in the foreseeable future Beijing has no mind to delineate the boundary and bury the border issue for good in the larger interest of bilateral harmony and regional calm. The principal reason underlying such an outlook is that Beijing thinks it gains leverage over New Delhi by having an unsettled border, which is being used as an instrument of inter-state relations.

While the carrot of settling the vexed issue "at an early date" through "mutual understanding and mutual accommodation" is routinely dangled, the stick of trouble on the border is never kept out of view. In recent years, this is the pattern that has been most in evidence.

In effect, what China is trying to tell India is that if New Delhi proceeds to deepen friendship with countries in Southeast Asia (most notably Vietnam, with which Beijing's relations have long been unhappy) and the Far East (Japan), then it can forget about border resolution.

The border issue is also a factor in China's relations with Pakistan. For both, their axis serves as a means to keep India off balance. If we look at the larger picture, not too much should be read into Beijing's supposed current disenchantment with Islamabad's inability to keep the Pakistan-based anti-China Islamic insurgents from harassing the People's Republic. For Beijing, Pakistan is of great nuisance value as far as India is concerned. It also gives the Chinese arrow-straight access to the seas in near proximity of the major oil-bearing regions of the world. From Islamabad's perspective, the unsettled Sino-Indian boundary is of capital value.

This game will be hard to pull off, but for China's conspicuous situational strengths. Its economy is about four times the size of India's, and its military capabilities easily outstrip those of this country. Besides, an expansionist appeal is historically built into the Chinese psyche. To compound matters, India is in the dubious position of having to be content with two hostile fronts simultaneously—with China and Pakistan.

When in the 1980s China had hinted at a territory swap with India, it had found itself under a degree of international isolation and had sought to overcome this handicap by seeking to build some understanding with India—then the leader of the non-aligned movement (NAM)—also with a view to raising its own profile with developing countries, which were mostly in NAM and formed a useful political bloc in the UN General Assembly.

Subsequently, this hint was obfuscated, and for the past 15 years Beijing has sought to give currency to the view-which some Indians have uncritically come to accept- that no Indian government is strong enough to engage in a territorial exchange with it—or is capable of doing so—to settle and normalise the boundary. This, in effect, is passing the buck.

The Modi government seems to have gone into the Chinese tango with inadequate preparation and an insufficient appreciation of the larger reality. This explains its recent over-exuberance when the Chinese leader was over.

Asian Age & The Deccan Chronicle, September 29, 2014